PRAIS

AFTER
ACTS

In *After Acts*, Bryan Litfin provides an engaging, critically informed, and edifying account of what early church traditions tell us about the major figures of the New Testament after the period described in the book of Acts. Through careful detective work, Litfin sifts history and legend to show what Christians today can learn from these important traditions.

MICHAEL GRAVES
Armerding Associate Professor of Old Testament, Wheaton College

The strength and integrity of what you find in these pages are rooted in Bryan Litfin's painstaking scholarship. But Bryan is no ordinary historian. He is also a preacher who loves to showcase the movements of divine grace through the events that we call history. Therefore, this book not only provides insight into the apostles; it also presents the glorious God whose hand continues to enliven men and women with apostolic faith.

CHRIS CASTALDO
Author of Talking with Catholics about the Gospel

Litfin has provided a fascinating survey of the "rest of the story" of the lives of the apostles (plus Mark, Luke, and Mary) beyond what we learn directly from the pages of Scripture itself. With a sure hand born of solid scholarly discernment concerning the extant historical documents and their varying reliability, he helps us to sift through fact and fantasy, and separate trustworthy traditions from fanciful embellishments. The results are realistic portraits that appropriately honor these great heroes of the faith (and their Lord) by confirming their redeemed humanity and their vibrant and courageous witness to the gospel.

RON MAN
Pastor of Worship/Missionary in Residence, First Evangelical Church, Memphis, Tennessee; Director, Worship Resources International

There has been a resurgence of interest in the past twenty years among evangelicals into the history and theology of the early Christian church. This has resulted in a number of scholarly monographs and collections of primary sources in translation. What is now happening, in large part due to the work of Dr. Bryan Litfin, is that such scholarly work is making its way into the hands of Christians in both the academy and in the church. *After Acts* continues that trajectory. Though erudite, it is written in a style and manner that is immediately accessible to all readers. Dr. Litfin tells a series of amazing stories, separating the wheat from the chaff in such a way that these disciples come alive once again. Dr. Litfin honors the Christian tradition but is not afraid to stand against the grain when the historical record demands it. Anyone interested in the men and women of the New Testament will find this book useful and fascinating.

GREG PETERS
Associate Professor of Medieval and Spiritual Theology, Torrey Honors Institute

Too often, contemporary discussions of extrabiblical data about the New Testament's main characters appeal to a vague entity called "early Christian tradition." In *After Acts*, Litfin does a great service by introducing ordinary readers to the actual sources in that tradition—in all of their glory and ambiguity—and explaining in a lively way how these things matter for ordinary Christians. The treasures laid bare by this book will delight anyone with a growing interest in the early church and its relationship to the New Testament.

STEPHEN T. PARDUE
Assistant Professor of Theology, Asia Graduate School of Theology (Manila)

Bryan Litfin has distinguished himself among evangelical theologians for his deep appreciation for the continuity of the faith that was once for all delivered to the saints. Adding to his growing list of books along these lines comes his latest: *After Acts: Exploring the Lives and Legends of the Apostles*. Illuminating for students, useful for pastors, accessible to everyone, this is an excellent introduction to the traditions that foreground the New Testament. Bryan traverses lots of territory and canvases a dizzying number of ancient sources to bring us this sure-footed, readable, and practical guide. If you're eager to grow in your appreciation for the characters who populate the pages of the New Testament—from Peter to Paul, James to John, Luke to Mary—I can think of no better place to start. Highly recommended!

TODD WILSON
Senior Pastor at Calvary Memorial Church

AFTER ACTS

EXPLORING THE LIVES AND LEGENDS OF THE APOSTLES

BRYAN M. LITFIN

MOODY PUBLISHERS
CHICAGO

© 2015 by
Bryan M. Litfin

Edited by Pam Pugh
Interior Design: Design Corps
Cover Design: Erik M. Peterson
Cover Image: The Crucifixion of St. Peter, 1600-01 (oil on panel), Caravaggio,
        Michelangelo Merisi da (1571-1610) / Santa Maria del Popolo, Rome,
        Italy / The Bridgeman Art Library

Library of Congress Cataloging-in-Publication Data

Litfin, Bryan M.
  After Acts : exploring the lives and legends of the apostles / Bryan Litfin.
    pages cm
  Summary: What happened to all those biblical figures once the Bible was finished? We've all heard it said: "According to early church tradition, Peter was crucified upside down," or "Paul went to Spain." Did Thomas found the Indian church? Or did Mary live in Ephesus? Were the twelve disciples all eventually martyred? Where do these ancient traditions come from, and how historically reliable are they? What is meant by the term "early church tradition"? *After Acts* opens up the world of the Bible right after it was written. Follow along with New Testament scholar Dr. Bryan Litfin as he explores the facts, myths, legends, archaeology, and questions of what happened in those most early days of Christianity. — Provided by publisher.
  Includes bibliographical references.
  ISBN 978-0-8024-1240-9 (paperback)
  1. Church history—Primitive and early church, ca. 30–600. I. Title.
BR162.3.L58 2015
270.1 — dc23

                                                2014034360

We hope you enjoy this book from Moody Publishers. Our goal is to provide high-quality, thought-provoking books and products that connect truth to your real needs and challenges. For more information on other books and products written and produced from a biblical perspective, go to www.moodypublishers.com or write to:

Moody Publishers
820 N. LaSalle Boulevard
Chicago, IL 60610

1 3 5 7 9 10 8 6 4 2

Printed in the United States of America

I dedicate this book to my daughter
Anna Elizabeth Litfin.

Because your soul magnifies the Lord,
and your spirit rejoices in God your Savior,
may He who is mighty do great things for you.

CONTENTS

TIMELINE OF
SIGNIFICANT DATES

Dates and life spans in black are best estimates.
Gray text and (?) indicate doubt on the author's
part that the event occurred at this time, if at all

Jesus Christ is resurrected
from the dead **33**

34 Paul is converted on
the road to Damascus

Peter first visits Rome (?) **40**

Mark turns back during Paul's
first missionary journey **46**

44 James the Great is martyred in Jerusalem;
Peter escapes from prison

James the Just presides over the church in
Jerusalem; Mark visits Alexandria (?);
Thomas evangelizes Edessa (and India?);
Bartholomew (?) and Judas Thaddeus (?)
evangelize in Syriac-speaking lands **50s**

49 Jerusalem council

57 Epistle to the Romans predicts Paul's
mission to Spain; Paul arrives in
Jerusalem and is arrested.

Paul departs for Rome but is shipwrecked on Malta for three months **59**

60 Paul arrives in Rome under house arrest and
soon writes his four Prison Epistles; Mark
composes his gospel under Peter's guidance

Luke writes his gospel, using Mark,
Q, and other texts as sources **61**

62 Paul is released from house arrest;
James the Just dies violently in Jerusalem;
Luke finishes Acts

Paul evangelizes Spain, ministers in the
Aegean, and writes 1 Timothy and Titus **63**

64 Great Fire of Rome; Paul returns to Rome

Core of Matthew's gospel composed at Antioch
under his leadership, using Mark, Q, and other
texts as sources; Paul writes 2 Timothy from
prison and is tried before Nero; Peter is executed
in Nero's circus and is buried on the Vatican Hill;
Mary dies and John arrives at Ephesus (?) **65**

66 Paul is executed and buried on the Ostian Road;
Jewish patriots in Judaea rebel against Rome

68 Emperor Nero dies;
John composes the initial version of
Revelation, based on his Patmos vision

Destruction of the Jewish temple
at Jerusalem by the Romans;
work begins on John's gospel (?) **70**

70s–
80s Luke ministers in Thebes (?);
Andrew ministers in Patras (?)

Book of Revelation
reaches its final form **95**

98 Philip the Evangelist (not the apostle) is
martyred and buried at Hierapolis (?);
Epistle of Clement

100 John's gospel reaches its final form

Ignatius of Antioch dies as a martyr in Rome **115**

130 Papias writes *Expositions of the Oracles of the Lord*

Trophy monument is erected over Peter's grave on the Vatican Hill **160**

165 Justin Martyr dies as a martyr in Rome

Irenaeus writes *Against Heresies* **180**

Hippolytus and Origen are actively writing; perpetual virginity of Mary begins to be emphasized; tomb of Thomas established at Edessa; *Acts of John; Acts of Thomas; Book of Thomas the Contender* **EARLY 3rd CENTURY**

196–212 Tertullian is actively writing late 2nd cent. Clement of Alexandria is actively writing; Polycrates is bishop of Ephesus; Dionysius is bishop of Corinth; trophy monument is erected over Paul's grave on the Ostian Road; Pantaenus visits southern India with the Christian message (?); *Muratorian Fragment* discusses the state of the biblical canon; *Acts of Peter; Acts of Paul; Acts of Andrew; Proto-Gospel of James; Gospel of Thomas*

Papyrus 45 attests to the collection of all four gospels in one manuscript **250**

258 Relics of Peter and Paul transferred to a catacomb on the Appian Road (?)

Life of Eusebius (*Church History* written in the late 200s/early 300s) **265–339**

LATE 3rd CENTURY Coffin in Thebes comes to be revered as Luke's

Constantine rises to power after his victory at the Milvian Bridge **312**

306–373 Life of Ephrem the Syrian

Council of Nicaea **325**

330s Small chapel erected over Paul's tomb on the Ostian Road (?); *Burying of the Martyrs* compiled (?)

Life of Jerome **347–419**

350 Completion of Old St. Peter's Basilica (?)

Life of Augustine **354–430**

349–407 Life of John Chrysostom

Epiphanius writes his antiheretical work *Panarion* **377**

Emperor Theodosius declares intent to build a new church over Paul's tomb on the Ostian Road **384**

381–384 Egeria goes on pilgrimage to Edessa

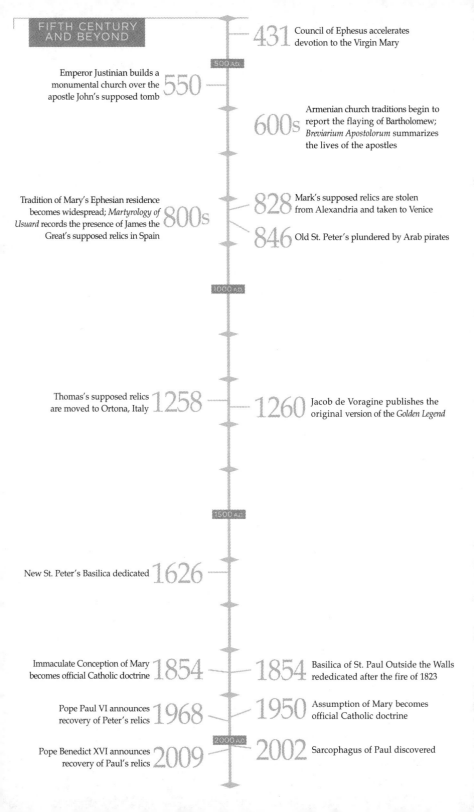

FIFTH CENTURY AND BEYOND

431 Council of Ephesus accelerates devotion to the Virgin Mary

Emperor Justinian builds a monumental church over the apostle John's supposed tomb **550**

500 A.D.

600s Armenian church traditions begin to report the flaying of Bartholomew; *Breviarium Apostolorum* summarizes the lives of the apostles

Tradition of Mary's Ephesian residence becomes widespread; *Martyrology of Usuard* records the presence of James the Great's supposed relics in Spain **800s**

828 Mark's supposed relics are stolen from Alexandria and taken to Venice

846 Old St. Peter's plundered by Arab pirates

1000 A.D.

Thomas's supposed relics are moved to Ortona, Italy **1258**

1260 Jacob de Voragine publishes the original version of the *Golden Legend*

1500 A.D.

New St. Peter's Basilica dedicated **1626**

Immaculate Conception of Mary becomes official Catholic doctrine **1854**

1854 Basilica of St. Paul Outside the Walls rededicated after the fire of 1823

Pope Paul VI announces recovery of Peter's relics **1968**

1950 Assumption of Mary becomes official Catholic doctrine

2000 A.D.

Pope Benedict XVI announces recovery of Paul's relics **2009**

2002 Sarcophagus of Paul discovered

TRACING THE TRADITION

"**P**eter was crucified upside down," you hear in a sermon, "according to tradition."

"Paul went to Spain," the pastor says on another day, "according to tradition."

Thomas founded the Indian church, Mary lived in Ephesus, the original apostles became martyrs—all according to this vague yet authoritative source called "early church tradition." But what exactly do we mean by this term? Where do these ancient traditions come from, and how reliable are they historically? If you have ever pondered such questions, keep reading. We are going to take a journey back to the ancient church.

WHO ARE WE CALLING APOSTLES?

As we proceed through this book, we will be investigating what happened to the apostles after the scriptural account of their lives came to an end, especially as recorded in the book of Acts. But to do this, we must first figure out what an apostle is. The word *apostolos* comes from a Greek verb meaning "to send out." In the original culture of ancient Greece, an apostle was just a sailor sent across the sea with no particular authority. Eventually the word came to mean a messenger or delegate.

First-century Judaism had its own Hebrew word for an official envoy who was commissioned to proclaim a precise message and who therefore possessed special authority—the *shaliah*. This seems to be the meaning behind the Greek word *apostolos* as it is used in the New Testament. The twelve disciples (or eleven, after Judas Iscariot's betrayal) were sent out by Jesus with the full authority of heaven (Matt. 10:1–3; 28:16–20). Over time, a few additional figures who were recognized as bearing the authoritative message of God likewise came to be included as apostles. The primary example is the apostle Paul, who was commissioned by the risen Lord (Acts 9:15; 22:21; 26:15–18; see also 1 Cor. 9:1; 15:8–9).

Yet the Bible refers to at least two other people as apostles: Barnabas (Acts 14:14) and James the Lord's brother (Gal. 1:19).[1] In the case of James, we know he witnessed a postresurrection appearance of Christ (1 Cor. 15:7). Although we have no record of this happening to Barnabas, perhaps he was one of the five hundred people who witnessed the risen Lord (1 Cor. 15:6). Normally, an apostle was someone who had been directly commissioned by Jesus Christ to proclaim the message of His saving death and resurrection.

A quick glance at our table of contents will reveal that not everyone listed there was an apostle in the technical sense. What factors guided my decision to include one figure and exclude another in this book? Though I intended the apostles to serve as the nucleus for our investigation, I also wanted to expand the list according to two criteria: the person's prominence in Scripture, and the existence of substantial historical traditions about him or her. Therefore I have included three personalities who were not biblical apostles: Mark, Luke, and Mary. I considered them too important to omit in a book like this, and we also have quite a bit of early church tradition about them. With these same criteria in mind, I have left out the replacement disciple Matthias (Acts 1:21–26) along with Barnabas, even though they both bore the title of apostle. And what about other New Testament characters such as Timothy, Titus, Philemon, or Jude? Since they were neither apostles nor prominent biblical personalities, I decided not to feature them in this book. Better to go deep on the main figures than to cover lots of names but only scratch the surface of each.

CLARIFYING TERMS

Church Fathers

Before we can begin our investigation into the postbiblical lives of the apostles, we need to be clear about some key concepts and presuppositions within the field of early Christian studies.[2] Anyone who digs into the traditions of the ancient church will immediately encounter a body of writers known collectively as the "church fathers." Who are we talking about here, and how should we think about them? While many other books (including one that I wrote) have made it their purpose to provide a thorough introduction to these foundational Christian figures, the present volume is not the place for that task. Nevertheless, a few general remarks must be made if we are to understand the academic study of early Christianity as it is practiced by contemporary scholars.

The term "church fathers" refers to the theologians, martyrs, bishops, and other ecclesiastical leaders who are considered to have been orthodox in their doctrine—as opposed to adhering to doctrine deemed heretical. Some of the most familiar church fathers include Clement of Rome, Ignatius of Antioch, Polycarp, Justin Martyr, Irenaeus, Tertullian, Clement of Alexandria, Origen, Cyprian, Eusebius of Caesarea, Athanasius, John Chrysostom, Gregory of Nazianzus, Augustine of Hippo, Ambrose of Milan, Jerome, and Cyril of Alexandria.

When we refer to the "church fathers," we are talking about men (and a few women) from the *ancient* period—that is to say, from the time of the Roman Empire until its fall to the barbarian invaders. So the time frame of the church fathers runs from the age of the biblical apostles until the end of antiquity. Since the ancient period came to a close around AD 500, we'll use that year as a rough cut-off date for the era of early Christianity.

Of course, the world didn't turn from ancient to medieval over-night, so depending on where the age of transition is established, some historians might add a few later figures to the list of church fathers. However, this term wouldn't normally describe Christian theologians from the high Middle Ages like Thomas Aquinas, nor anyone from subsequent historical eras, such as Martin Luther, John Calvin, or Jonathan Edwards.

Orthodox and Heretical

In defining these ancient fathers, we have noted that the judg-ment of church history has found them to be *orthodox*, a word that literally means "adhering to right belief or doctrine." Most evangelical Christians would aspire to be orthodox in this sense of the term. And if we have any desire to be connected to a broader tradition that has come down to us through the ages, we will want to think of ourselves as tracing our spiritual roots and having a connection to our spiritual ancestors. In the ancient period, the Christians who held essentially the same faith as ours are the ones whom we have designated "church fathers."

However, the definition of orthodoxy is a topic of great debate in the contemporary field of early Christian studies. The prob-lem is, whose orthodoxy are we talking about? Today, the term "Christianity"—though expressed in numerous manifestations across the globe—is unified around the basic proclamation that Jesus of Nazareth is God in the flesh who died on a cross and rose again for salvation. It is one thing though, to look back from the vantage point of established Christianity and determine who and what was orthodox by today's standards, and quite another to actually live in the age when no single viewpoint had yet gained the upper hand. In such a context, one person's orthodoxy is another's heresy. Who gets to define the truth?

In light of this definition problem, many modern scholars reject the division of ancient persons or texts into the categories of "orthodox church fathers" and "heretical sects." These scholars believe there was no such thing as an original form of Christianity that Jesus actually taught, or a Holy Book to lay down the divine standard of truth. Instead, they say, there were multiple Christianities, each comprising people who interpreted their own sacred texts as they pleased, and trying hard to trump the other guy's view of Jesus. Most of these Christianities are lost today because one main form of the religion emerged as triumphant.

However, in ancient times—so these modern scholars say— many other "Christian" messages existed. For example, some "Christians" said Jesus was just an ordinary human being who followed the Jewish law better than anyone else and taught salvation by works. Other "Christians" interpreted Jesus as a mystical revealer from the heavenly realm whose body was not real and who did not actually die by crucifixion. And a third type of "Christianity" is the type we know today—but it was just one of many different varieties of the faith in ancient times. The only reason it won was because it employed devious scheming and power politics. In other words, the Christian faith as we know it does not exist because it is true but because it was clever and manipulative.[3]

Liberal and Conservative

The issues I am describing here all go back to how one views the Bible. Is it the divine revelation of God's will for mankind? Or is it just the product of human religious instincts, a collection of writings cobbled together as ancient people fought to establish their views? The way one answers these questions creates something of a divide in the field of early Christian studies. Though the terminology is imperfect, we can, generally speaking, distinguish between scholars who are "liberal" and "conservative." These terms do not describe a political outlook. Rather, they categorize two approaches to the Bible that are not easy to describe with any other terminology.

A biblical conservative understands the Old and New Testaments to be authored by people who were inspired by God Himself, which means that whatever is recorded in Scripture must be true and accurate in a meaningful sense. A liberal, in contrast, considers the biblical writings as important historical documents, though written by human hands only, and therefore prone to errors or even falsifications.

I am definitely a conservative. This approach affects how I handle biblical texts as historical evidence. I assume Scripture will always be true, and I will never doubt God's Word. Even so, there is a wide range of potential views within this general belief system. To say a biblical statement is "true" means it is accurate according to the way an ancient person would have looked at the world. It is always hard to lift ourselves from our own point of view, but if we can achieve it, we will see that modern people think differently than the ancients did about written texts and their proper uses. For example, we tend to feel a much stronger need to report objective facts in strict chronological order. Ancient people had looser expectations for how historical documents were supposed to function. So, while I will always treat Scripture as inerrant, I will also understand it as the ancient work that it truly is. My approach will take into account that the Bible reflects its original culture's setting and assumptions. At the same time, I will operate with the overarching belief that errors about timeless truth, or intentional misrepresentation from the author, are not found within Scripture.

Gnosticism

Applying these interpretive principles to the definition of orthodoxy means the Bible is the final standard of right belief. It alone records the true theology of the Christian faith, and whatever deviates from biblical doctrine must be wrong. Therefore, to believe in biblical orthodoxy means there is also such a thing as heresy.

Take, for example, the people I mentioned above who viewed Jesus as a revealer from beyond whose body was not real. I was referring to the heretical movement called Gnosticism.

Because we know so little about the ancient Gnostic sects, it isn't easy to define an essential bottom line that characterizes all Gnostics. For this reason, some scholars don't even want to use the term anymore. But I don't think we need to be quite that skeptical. While not denying serious difficulties of definition, we can still recognize that many ancient people who claimed to be followers of Jesus understood His message to focus on secret knowledge (*gnosis*) that would help the human soul trapped in the evil material world ascend to a higher degree of union with the divine. Though there are many different permutations of that basic Gnostic message, it does represent a definable point of view held by real people and contained in specific writings.

Since Gnosticism is a recognizable point of view, we are able to compare and contrast it with other perspectives. And when we do, we discover it isn't equivalent to the message that the Son of God died on the cross and rose bodily for our salvation. To equate these two outlooks is as ridiculous as saying the two messages of "higher taxes for more government programs" and "lower taxes for greater individual freedom" are simply two facets of an imaginary philosophy called *taxism*. We could perhaps make up a term like *taxism*, but because it is far too broad in its definition—to the point of including contradictory perspectives!—it is so confusing as to be meaningless. These are actually two distinct views of taxation, not a single philosophy.

In the same way, it makes little sense to define *early Christianity* as including every ancient person who liked Jesus and claimed to follow Him. We should instead make a clear demarcation between groups that proclaimed one message about Him or another. And if we want to be historically accurate here, we should let the earliest known proclamation about Jesus define the term *Christianity*—namely, the message that Jesus was the Lord, the Christ, and the Son of God who died and rose again.

So what can we say about the Gnostics? Were they just one of the many ancient "Christianities"? Or did they represent a deviation from the true Christian faith? Now our question of "orthodoxy vs. heresy" has been brought into sharp focus—and here is my answer. Though the Gnostics called themselves Christians, their core beliefs were demonstrably different from the earliest proclamation about Jesus in the decades after His historical life. That is why I believe it makes no sense to identify them as Christians.

And I am not alone in this view. Generally speaking, most conservatives would identify true Christianity with the orthodox apostles and church fathers, which means Gnosticism is a heresy by definition. On the other hand, many liberals would be open to treating alternate religious creeds like Gnosticism as just another form of early Christianity, since the Gnostics themselves claimed to be followers of Jesus.

In this book, however, I will take the side of those who identify the apostles and their successors (the church fathers) with authentic Christianity. That being said, I will also discuss any valid historical evidence about the apostles that can be gleaned from the writings of the heretical sects. Taken together, the writings of the church fathers and the heretics—as well as some texts that blur the differences between them—are our primary means of discerning what happened to the apostles after Acts.

THE SOURCES BEHIND THE TRADITION

Earlier, we raised the question of exactly what we mean by "tradition." Is there some unified voice of church history whose authority is so venerable and supreme that we must obey it? In reality, the historical sources of ancient tradition are far messier than that. To address this matter, let us first distinguish between the Protestant and Catholic understandings of tradition.

For Catholics, the concept of church tradition refers to a second source of divine revelation—in addition to the Bible—that has come down to us through the teaching ministry of the bishops.

The Catholic Church "receives and venerates with an equal affection of piety and reverence" the written Scripture and the unwritten traditions passed down from Christ to the apostles and their successors who lead the church.[4] Or again, the Catholic Church declares that "sacred theology rests on the written word of God, together with sacred tradition, as its primary and perpetual foundation."[5]

Protestants, on the other hand, hold to the principle of *sola Scriptura*, or Scripture alone. This means official church tradition does not possess the same authority as the Bible, nor does it stand as a judge over biblical interpretation. At most, tradition can serve as a helpful guide. The sources about Christianity from the ancient period (or any other time, for that matter) are important and valuable as historical records, yet they are not equal to the inspired Word of God. This is the viewpoint taken in the present book.

What, then, are the historical sources about the apostles? A lot of material is found among the medieval legends that cropped up long after the apostolic age had ended. These legends appear in a variety of genres, from miracle-filled biographies and martyr stories to formal liturgies and hymns. Considered as a whole, this type of literature is known as hagiography, or "writings about holy people."

Eventually some of the traditional anecdotes about the apostles were gathered into martyrologies, which were ecclesiastical catalogs that kept track of the annual feast days for various martyrs and saints. Because this information was announced regularly in church, the legends of the apostles became well known. Many of the most cherished hagiographical stories were collected and published by the Italian bishop Jacobus de Voragine in his *Golden Legend*, which became a wildly popular bestseller in the late Middle Ages. In this way the heroic tales of the apostles were disseminated to the masses, and everyone believed they were true.

However, from a scholarly perspective, the medieval sources have very little historical value except insofar as they reproduce earlier texts. As a general rule, historians will privilege earlier sources because they were closer to the actual events. One of my operating assumptions in the present book is that if an assertion about an apostle doesn't have any early evidence to back it up, it probably didn't happen. My historical decisions will revolve around finding *early attestation from multiple reliable sources.*

Back to the Early Church Fathers

So then, as we turn our attention to these ancient sources, we must first listen to the witness of the early church fathers. These writers were, by and large, the pastors and theologians who ministered to the people of God. Though they did not always demonstrate a critical and discerning eye, and sometimes repeated tall tales they had heard, they can still serve as valuable historical witnesses about the apostles, especially when a claim is attested by more than one church father.

We should pay particularly close attention to the writers from the second and third centuries because they were not far removed from the apostolic age. Examples of such figures include Clement of Rome, Papias, Justin Martyr, Irenaeus, Tertullian, Clement of Alexandria, and Origen. These writers are important because they made it their business to pass on what they had learned about the apostles from earlier generations.

Eusebius's *Church History*

However, the most important voice among the orthodox church fathers is Eusebius of Caesarea, who wrote the first surviving historical study of Christianity in the late third and early fourth century. Like other writers of his day, Eusebius was sometimes gullible and prone to pious exaggeration. Yet that does not mean his *Church History* is just a lot of conjecture. Eusebius often made sure he gathered historical documents and supported his assertions by quoting from earlier writings. He was able to do this because he had access to the best possible records from the impressive ecclesiastical library that had been established at Caesarea on the coast of Palestine.

Caesarea had recently been home to the greatest scholar of the ancient church, Origen (d. 251), whose immense intellect made this city famous for Christian scholarship. The library's collection was then augmented by Eusebius's studious mentor, Pamphilus. If historical records about the origins of the church could be found anywhere, they could be found at Caesarea. Eusebius mined them freely, rounding out his narrative with letters he obtained from other congregations, or from his own personal travels and research. For this reason, the *Church History* of Eusebius is one of our most precious historical sources about Christianity in the ancient period.

New Testament Apocrypha

In addition to the writings of individual church fathers, a large body of anonymous texts has come down to us from ancient times. These writings are normally referred to as "New Testament apocrypha."[6] Numerous literary genres are represented here, including various types of gospels about Jesus, dialogues between biblical characters, dramatic revelations of heavenly or end-times events, hymns and liturgies, collections of wise sayings, forged letters, and even heroic stories about the apostles. Often these texts have survived only in fragmentary form. Some contain teachings of dubious acceptability, making them quasi-heretical. That is to say, their spiritual outlook puts them in a theological grey area between orthodoxy and heresy.

The apocryphal texts appear to have been read by mainline Christians and sectarians alike, though the church fathers frequently expressed their suspicions about these works. Of course, some ancient writings about Jesus and the apostles clearly came from heretical circles, such as the Nag Hammadi Library, a collection of Gnostic texts discovered in the sands of Egypt in 1945.

Yet poor theology doesn't automatically mean every historical point is wrong. The New Testament apocrypha are useful texts that may provide clues about the postbiblical lives of the apostles. But here again, this evidence will need to be as *early* and *reliable* as possible. When we encounter later traditions that contain not just supernatural events but fantastic legends and grandiose spectacles, we will need to be more circumspect in our historical assessments. Furthermore, to be considered as valid evidence, the narrated events must fit squarely into the period being described instead of reflecting the piety of a later generation. The apocryphal material does not always observe this rule, so it must be used with caution.

Buried Treasure

One final source of evidence can be mentioned briefly. Along with the written historical testimony, we can sometimes gain knowledge about the apostles from the veneration of their tombs and the collection of their bones. Honorable burial was important to the Jews and early Christians alike. Over time, devotion to the tombs of the martyrs developed into a full-blown cult of the saints—a religious system of veneration and pilgrimage that centered on the relics of holy individuals. Of course, the apostles would be considered especially holy, so we can sometimes determine where they may have ministered by tracking their bones back to their original resting place. In this book we will occasionally look at the archaeological evidence about the tombs of the apostles, particularly with respect to Peter and Paul.

ANCIENT SOURCES FOR MODERN TIMES

Before we finally dive into our investigation of individual apostles, I want to explain how to engage firsthand with the historical sources we are about to study. Whenever possible, I will quote from the widely used collection of ancient Christian texts called the Ante-Nicene Fathers and the Nicene and Post-Nicene Fathers.

Although this thirty-eight-volume library does not represent the most recent academic scholarship, it has the great advantage of being available online at www.ccel.org/fathers.html. I will typically provide citations within the text to the ANF or the NPNF 1 or 2 (it was issued in two series), along with the volume number and a reference to the particular work.

The writings of the Jewish historian Josephus can likewise be found at www.ccel.org/ccel/josephus/complete. Alternatively, some texts that do not appear in the ANF/NPNF library can be found at www.earlychristianwritings.com. And of course, many other ancient documents are found in random places on the web. As often as possible, I encourage you to take the time to read these texts for yourself online. This may help to demystify the great and mysterious authority called "early church tradition."

But if you do happen to look up a few things, be sure and share them with your pastor—he may want to include them in his next sermon!

CHAPTER 1

MATTHEW

Whether in ancient times or modern, human beings are capable of great evil. Yet none is beyond redemption.

Eighteenth-century pastor John Newton was once a slave-trader, which meant he was involved in one of the most heinous travesties the earth has ever known. This was a man whose daily treatment of his fellow human beings was abusive and unjust. Only later did Newton come to realize what a blind and wandering wretch he truly was. His sense of awe at God's sweet mercy and forgiveness inspired him to write the beloved hymn "Amazing Grace."

If the timeline of history were different, perhaps the biblical disciple Matthew would have appreciated John Newton's great hymn. Matthew was a tax collector, a profession notorious in ancient times for its abusive practices. In fact, a genuine form of enslavement was being perpetrated against the Jews through excessive taxes. Yet when Jesus of Nazareth showed up at the tax booth, Matthew's life—like Newton's—was suddenly diverted down a new path toward freedom and redemption. So what did Matthew do with the bountiful forgiveness he found in Christ? In other words, what did he accomplish for his Savior after Acts?

To answer that question, we must first understand who Matthew was before he discovered the amazing grace of God.

THE COLLABORATOR IS CALLED

During Matthew's lifetime, his homeland of Galilee was controlled by the Romans through the puppet ruler Herod Antipas. The foreign overlords demanded two things of their subjects: peace and taxes. Yet the job of tax collection didn't originally belong to the Roman government like our IRS today. Instead, aristocratic capitalists called *publicans* formed tax-collecting businesses. Though these big shots operated out of Rome or the provincial capitals, local tax gatherers from the nearby population provided the necessary "boots on the ground" at each collection point.

Matthew was a man like this—a Jewish collaborator with Rome's appointee, Herod Antipas, who levied heavy taxes to fund his many building projects. Obviously the traitors who helped Antipas would be resented by those who had to hand over their hard-earned wealth. Sellouts like Matthew were agents of the oppressive Roman regime, often getting filthy rich by overcharging the little guy. The Jews hated the publicans in general, but they especially despised the local Jewish representatives who carried out the actual process of examining goods and exacting taxes. Such people were lumped with other "sinners" as hardly worthy of being considered Jews—until Jesus came along and offered Matthew a new life.

The calling of Matthew as a disciple of Jesus is recounted in the Synoptic Gospels (i.e., the three gospels that outline their story the same way—Matthew, Mark, and Luke). Mark's gospel puts it like this:

> [Jesus] went out again beside the sea, and all the crowd was coming to him, and he was teaching them. And as he passed by, he saw *Levi the son of Alphaeus* sitting at the tax

booth, and he said to him, "Follow me." And he rose and followed him. And as he reclined at table in his house, many tax collectors and sinners were reclining with Jesus and his disciples, for there were many who followed him. And the scribes of the Pharisees, when they saw that he was eating with sinners and tax collectors, said to his disciples, "Why does he eat with tax collectors and sinners?" And when Jesus heard it, he said to them, "Those who are well have no need of a physician, but those who are sick. I came not to call the righteous, but sinners." (Mark 2:13–17, italics added.)

This account, like Luke's version, calls the tax-collecting disciple "Levi." Matthew's gospel, however, changes the name to "Matthew" (9:9). Apparently this disciple went by two names. When the gospel of Matthew was written, his identity needed to be clarified so everyone could see that the man writing the story was one and the same as the despicable tax collector. This demonstrates that the early Christians weren't shy about reading a biography of Jesus attributed to a notorious sinner. Just the opposite—Matthew's sinfulness is highlighted in the text. Yet due to his transformation by the Lord, he was able to write the ancient church's most widely read gospel account!

As a tax agent, Matthew would have been literate in both Aramaic and Greek. He was no peasant laborer but a businessman who worked for Gentile bosses, kept careful records, and wrote out customs slips. The Bible portrays him as having a very nice home with a dining room large and well-furnished enough for many other rich men to gather there. Yet underneath all the trappings of wealth, Matthew may have felt pangs of guilt. Here was a man who, instead of commiserating with his countrymen, joined an abusive system and worked the angles to profit at the expense of his fellow Jews.

The place where Matthew's traitorous work took place was Capernaum on the Sea of Galilee. But unbeknownst to him, Jesus had decided to make this little fishing village the home base of His ministry in fulfillment of a prophecy from Isaiah (Matt. 4:12–17). Capernaum was also the probable hometown of Peter. We can imagine Matthew living a life of considerable comfort here, yet always having to bear the burden of social rejection. For that reason he was ripe for the harvest when Jesus issued the call, "Follow me."

Abandoning his life as a tax collector, Matthew became one of Jesus' inner circle, the Twelve. He lived and ate and prayed with his Rabbi on a daily basis. Then, after the Romans crucified Jesus on the cross of Calvary, Matthew was one of those who witnessed the risen Lord (1 Cor. 15:5) and saw Him ascend into heaven (Acts 1:1–14). From this point on, Matthew disappears from further mention in the Bible. Yet he is known by all Christians today because of his one great legacy to the church: he wrote the first gospel in the New Testament.

Or did he?

MATTHEW WRITING MATTHEW

For many years—centuries, even—the church believed Matthew wrote the first of the four gospels. The canonical order of Matthew, Mark, Luke, and John is familiar to anyone who has ever cracked open the Good Book. Yet despite this long tradition, most scholars today don't consider this order of authorship to be correct. Only a few conservatives still defend it, while many other conservatives do not, along with the majority of liberals (refer to the introduction for clarification of these approaches).

The Synoptic Problem

The questions of when Matthew's gospel was written, and according to what sources, and in what relation to the other gospels, are all part of the complex academic debate called the Synoptic Problem. The issue arises because Matthew, Mark, and Luke are so alike in their wording and outlook that mere coincidence cannot explain these similarities; yet it is extremely difficult to reconstruct the exact literary relationship between the three works. Scholars have put forth many complicated theories about how the Synoptic Gospels came to be.

Fortunately for us, an in-depth examination of this problem goes beyond the topics we are addressing in this book. Though we will touch on a few key synoptic issues, we want to focus instead on what the apostles did for Christ's kingdom after our inspired record of them comes to an end. In the case of the apostle Matthew, ancient tradition doesn't tell us much about his later life. Though we will examine those traditional accounts in a moment, the early church has mainly remembered Matthew for one preeminent deed: his authorship of the gospel that bears his name. But since many modern scholars doubt even this, what are we to believe? Did the greedy tax collector who was so radically transformed by the call of Jesus actually pen the first gospel? Without delving into all the complexities of the Synoptic Problem, we should at least try and determine whether the apostle Matthew can rightly be considered a New Testament author.

Papias

The earliest mention of Matthew (and remember: in studying history, earlier accounts tend to be the most reliable) comes from an ancient church father named Papias of Hierapolis. The city of Hierapolis was no small village but a bustling metropolis famous for its hot springs, which drew visitors from far and wide. Even today, people still come to modern Pamukkale, Turkey, to visit them. In Colossians 4:12–13 we read that a Christian church had been planted there through the ministry of Epaphras in nearby Colossae (see also Col. 1:6–7). So when Papias was pastoring the congregation at Hierapolis in the early second century, his city had a rich ecclesial tradition going all the way back to the apostolic age.

Papias himself states that whenever church leaders came to visit, he always asked for their recollections about anything the Lord's disciples ever said or did (NPNF2, vol. 1, *Church History* 3.39.2–4). Apparently Papias was a man who made it his business to know what the earliest apostles had been up to. Therefore, one of his statements preserved by the later church historian Eusebius is very relevant to our inquiry. Papias declared: "Matthew wrote the oracles in the Hebrew language, and everyone [translated] them as he was able" (*C.H.* 3.39.16).[1] The meaning of this statement is hotly contested by scholars today. The Greek word for "oracles" is *logia*, or sayings, but what exactly does that mean? The most plausible view is that it was a collection of sayings Jesus Himself uttered in Aramaic—and who better to compile such a text than an educated and detail-oriented Jew like Matthew who was in Jesus' inner circle?

The Q-Source

As it turns out, Matthew's gospel actually does provide strong evidence of having used a collection of Jesus' sayings as one of its sources. We can infer this because Luke's gospel, though written in a different time and place, has preserved much of the same material. Luke displays close affinities to Matthew in his presentation of Jesus' teachings, often using exactly the same wording. However, most scholars believe that neither of these writers was dependent on the other.[2] If this is so, they must have both had access to a shared "sayings source" that they used to fill out their narratives. Borrowing from a common text is the only plausible explanation for two independent authors recording almost exactly the same material in their respective works.

Indeed, an editorial process like this is to be expected from good historians. Luke states outright that he used written eyewitness sources (Luke 1:1–4). Apparently one of these was a text or dossier that is now lost, yet is partially preserved in Matthew and Luke. The scholars in Germany who advanced this theory called the collection of sayings *Quelle*, or Source, and today it is abbreviated as Q. Could this ancient document (or more likely, a collection of documents in various editions) have grown out of the handwritten notes captured by one of Jesus' most grateful disciples as he sat at his Master's feet? The suggestion is intriguing.

Unfortunately, the hypothetical collection called Q has not survived today as a separate text, so we cannot say exactly what was in it—or even for certain that it existed. However, since Jewish disciples often captured the wise sayings of their rabbis, and since the church father Papias had heard that Matthew served as a scribal recorder of Jesus' *logia*, it is at least plausible that the Q-source did exist, and that it originally had a Matthean core.

Mark as a Source

What is interesting about the gospels of Matthew and Luke, however, is that they don't just use Q as a common source. They also use Mark. About 95 percent of Mark is reproduced in Matthew or Luke in some form, though the elements of the narrative are moved around, amplified, abbreviated, or polished into better Greek style. Themes that would have been especially important to Jewish-Christians[3]— such as the hostility of Israel's national leaders to the teachings of Jesus—are developed by Matthew. On the other hand, historically irrelevant material is pruned away. For example, the side note explaining Jewish customs in Mark 7:3–4 is omitted as unnecessary in Matthew 15:1–2.

Matthew's Audience

All of this points to a Jewish-Christian audience for Matthew's gospel. It was written by a well-educated Jewish man with urban sensibilities, using Mark and a collection of Jesus' sayings as its main sources. This means it wasn't the first gospel written. It was at least the second; and as we will see in chapter 3, it was probably the third (after Luke).

On the face of things, then, it would seem the apostle Matthew has given the church a gospel that shapes its narrative to highlight the Jewishness of Jesus. Even if this wasn't the earliest of the four gospels, it is still a precious treasure that celebrates Israel's Messiah in a unique way.

Yet this historical reconstruction of the book's authorship raises an interesting question: Why would an eyewitness of the Lord like Matthew use a non-eyewitness author like Mark as the basis of his account? To many modern observers, this is a very big problem. In fact, scholars in the liberal camp typically *deny* that the disciple Matthew wrote the gospel that bears his name—and one of the main reasons is its use of Mark, which is thought to be inexplicable for an apostle who actually saw Jesus. Other arguments for non-Matthean authorship include the gospel's more developed theology, which is believed to reflect Jewish-Christian relations at a later time than when Matthew would have been writing; and also its excellent Greek prose, suggesting a better education than would be expected for a Galilean tax collector. What are we to make of such seemingly radical claims?

THE GOSPEL "ACCORDING TO" MATTHEW

As we consider the question of Matthean authorship, let us first recall that the ancient church has always attributed this gospel to Matthew. By the second century—and probably very early in that century—the titles of the four canonical gospels had been settled and were included with the books. All the surviving manuscripts of Matthew's gospel name him in the title (except a few that are so tattered, we can't be certain of the ascribed author). Furthermore, the church fathers unanimously agree that Matthew was the author of a gospel.

Matthew's Languages

Following the lead of Papias, we find Irenaeus of Lyons saying, "Matthew also issued a written Gospel among the Hebrews in their own dialect, while Peter and Paul were preaching at Rome, and laying the foundations of the church"—that is, during the 60s AD (ANF, vol. 1, *Against Heresies* 3.1.1). Likewise, Origen of

Alexandria reports, "Among the four Gospels, which are the only indisputable ones in the Church of God under heaven, I have learned by tradition that the first was written by Matthew, who was once a publican, but afterwards an apostle of Jesus Christ, and it was prepared for the converts from Judaism, and published in the Hebrew language" (NPNF2, vol. 1, *C.H.* 6.25.4). Thus, according to widespread ancient church recollections, Matthew published a gospel for Jewish-Christians in their own language (which would have been Aramaic, a sister language to Hebrew).

But as we have seen, the biblical gospel of Matthew was almost certainly composed in Greek. What prompted these statements about an Aramaic version? The fact is, an Aramaic gospel (or gospels) linked to Matthew's name did circulate in antiquity. However, the inspired Greek text in the New Testament was not a direct translation of any such work. On the other hand, that doesn't mean Aramaic writings couldn't have served as historical sources for our inspired text. The evidence suggests the biblical gospel of Matthew was the result of a complex editorial process in which a variety of sources were stitched together—including the original Aramaic sayings of the Lord Jesus Christ, translated into Greek.

Matthew's Editorial Team

To carry out this complicated literary task, there is a distinct possibility that Matthew did not work alone but assigned the writing of his gospel to a church community under his direction. Such a process wouldn't have been foreign to the concept of authorship in antiquity, since the ancients cared more about the authority behind a book than the exact method of its production.

We should picture the editorial work being performed by a Jewish-Christian congregation in which the apostle was prominent and respected, yet other capable scribes were available to help shape the final version of the narrative. Matthew, the authoritative eyewitness of the Lord, would have been the driving force behind the publication process, even if other Christians may have put some personal touches on the final product.

Many conservative scholars are willing to grant that the gospel's central Matthean core—his eyewitness remembrances, recorded sayings of Jesus, and major narrative themes—was nonetheless shaped and molded over time by Matthew's community to give us the text we now have. This does not contradict anything stated in the Word of God. We would simply understand that the Holy Spirit's ministry of inspiration guided any writers who helped produce our Scripture. Yet behind it all, the early church fathers recognized Matthew's essential contribution to the book—including his use of original Aramaic sources—and rightly credited its authorship to him.

So, then, perhaps we might imagine that the literary efforts of Matthew looked something like this. An initial version of the gospel was composed by a gifted Greek stylist under Matthew's leadership in the mid-60s. This would have been before the destruction of the Jewish temple, which explains why some verses assume its continued existence. Why would Matthew decide to preserve Jesus' command to leave sacrificial gifts before the altar (5:24) or his affirmation that God dwells within the temple (23:21), if the church now knew the temple had been obliterated by the Romans? There are many good reasons to think the bulk of Matthew's work happened before AD 70, the year the temple was destroyed. And yet, after this initial effort was complete, we can suppose some further editing may have taken place to help later Christians understand their situation in the post-70 world.[4]

Matthew's Sources

As all good historians should do, Matthew used whatever textual evidence he had at his disposal. One of his most important sources was the collection of Jesus' sayings that may have grown out of his own note-taking efforts in Aramaic. In addition, Matthew surely would have held Peter, with his bold personality and obvious closeness to Jesus, in high esteem as the leader of the Twelve. Therefore Matthew structured his work around the gospel that Peter's assistant Mark had recently composed at Rome (see chapter 2).

In light of the ancient church's desire to preserve the unity of its proclamation about Jesus, the use of Mark is not only plausible, it is extremely likely. Relying especially on these two sources (Q and Mark), along with his own personal memories and any other sources available to him, Matthew employed a skilled writer to compose a gospel that suited the needs of his Jewish-Christian congregation.

Matthew's Home Base

Where did all of this writing and editing take place? Since it must have occurred at a major intellectual center with a substantial Jewish population, the most commonly suggested location is Syrian Antioch. We know the apostle Peter, who plays an especially prominent role in Matthew's gospel, had been a respected and influential leader there (Gal. 2:11–14; and see chapter 9 on Peter). It would make sense for Matthew to highlight this well-known figure from his own Antiochian church (and from his hometown of Capernaum!).

The book of Acts also depicts a large Jewish-Christian community in Antioch, very devoted to Hebraic customs, yet possessing a zeal for Gentile evangelism. This profile dovetails with the themes emphasized in Matthew, such as the Great Commission to go into all the world, baptizing and making disciples (28:18–20). Furthermore, the later bishop at Antioch named Ignatius, who ministered in the early second century, reflects awareness of Matthew's text in his letters. All this to say, the gospel of Matthew fits perfectly with the type of congregation we know existed in Antioch. Though we cannot be 100 percent certain, we can imagine a writing like this being intended for Antiochian believers. At the same time, the inspiration of the Holy Spirit ensured that the gospel's message was timelessly relevant to all generations.

THE SINNER PENS A CLASSIC

The gospel of Matthew is this apostle's greatest legacy. Although some obscure church legends try to give Matthew a pious concern for evangelism by describing his missionary journeys to various lands, scholars today put little credence in those late-appearing accounts. For example, an early medieval text incorrectly attributed to a certain Babylonian bishop named Abdias recounts Matthew's daring exploits and miraculous adventures in the land of Ethiopia (Pseudo-Abdias, book 6). A Matthean ministry in Ethiopia is also attested by the church father Rufinus in his Latin translation and updating of Eusebius's historical work (*Ecclesiastical History* 10.9). Although this Ethiopian destination for Matthew is doubtful because the idea didn't emerge until around AD 400, it has nonetheless entered official Catholic tradition in the text called the Roman Martyrology, which is still used liturgically today.

Other sources link Matthew with various locales such as Parthia or Persia. Yet another story situates him in an unknown city called Myrna, inhabited by a race of cannibals whose persecutions led to his death (ANF, vol. 8, *Acts and Martyrdom of St. Matthew the Apostle*; see also the *Acts of Andrew and Matthias*, where the replacement disciple Matthias may be confused with Matthew). Any reader of these texts will quickly discern they are legendary and devoid of accurate historical detail. As opposed to the careful and meticulous way that the canonical gospels unfold their narratives, these apocryphal texts jump straight into fantastic tales that have the obvious ring of later church piety.

On the other hand, the testimony of Eusebius is much less speculative: "Matthew, who had at first preached to the Hebrews, when he was about to go to other peoples, committed his Gospel to writing in his native tongue" (NPNF2, vol. 1, *C.H.* 3.24.6). Here we see again the tradition that Matthew wrote in Aramaic and was associated with Jewish-Christian circles. However, the precise identity of the "other peoples" to whom he supposedly ministered is lost in the sands of time. Nobody close to the apostle's own lifetime recorded what he did. We have no historically solid traditions about Matthew's missionary journeys or his martyrdom. The most we can say is that he was likely involved in evangelizing Aramaic-speaking Jews, probably around Antioch.

Thus, what the apostle Matthew actually accomplished for Jesus was not to travel around the empire defeating pagan opponents but to craft and produce the New Testament gospel that bears his name. Like the slaver-turned-preacher John Newton who composed a glorious hymn, Matthew, the former tax extortionist, received the great privilege of writing the very words of Scripture. The pen that once kept false and abusive ledger books was used instead to record the greatest story ever told. Now *that* is amazing grace!

REPORT CARD

MATTHEW		
Ministered in Antioch	B
Published a Jewish-Christian gospel in Aramaic	C-
Led a Jewish-Christian congregation	B+
Took notes that were used in the composition of his biblical gospel	A-
Directly shaped the composition of his biblical gospel	A
Wrote his biblical gospel by himself	B-
Went on evangelistic missions to Ethiopia or cannibalistic tribes	F

A= Excellent, B= Good, C= Average, D= Below average, F= Not passing

MARK

One of the foremost sights in the great city of Venice—in addition to its famous canals—is the cathedral of San Marco, known in English as St. Mark's. What does this ornate Italian building have to do with the first-century gospel writer? Medieval accounts assert that certain crafty merchants of Venice stole the bones of the evangelist Mark in AD 828 from their resting place in Alexandria, Egypt, and placed them in the cathedral. This in turn raises the question of why Mark's bones would have been in Egypt in the first place. After he disappeared from the biblical narrative, did he go to Alexandria to write the gospel that bears his name? Mark had failed in his first attempt at ministry. Judging only from the book of Acts, we wouldn't have much reason to think this wishy-washy assistant to the apostles would have had anything positive to contribute to the church. But as we are about to see, the young John Mark was a man who got one of life's rare privileges: a second chance.

THE COMEBACK KID

We all love a good comeback story. In such tales, the young upstart rises like a meteor, fails big, then fights back against the odds to win the victory. Tech whiz Steve Jobs was like that. After producing the wildly popular Apple Macintosh, he tried to stage a coup against his CEO and was fired. But when he found his way back to Apple, he presided over the rise of the ubiquitous iPod, iPhone, and iPad—products that revolutionized the world.

Or take Henry Ford. Despite a promising start working for Thomas Edison, when Ford struck out on his own, his new car companies fizzled. Only when the Model T came out did sales skyrocket and make Ford an automotive mogul. Today his name is plastered on millions of cars around the world.

In biblical times, John Mark was also something of a comeback kid like this. Everything looked positive for him at first. He was a Jew from Jerusalem, the son of a woman named Mary whose house had become the apostles' base of operations in the city (Acts 12:12). Mary seems to have been one of Peter's close associates because he rushed to her home as soon as he was released from prison. The household was large and wealthy enough to have a servant girl as a gatekeeper. In addition to this promising pedigree on his mother's side, Mark was also the cousin of Barnabas, one of Paul's primary coworkers. All of this would suggest that Mark had a bright future in Christian ministry.

Disappointing Start

Recognizing the youth's potential, Paul and Barnabas brought Mark with them to Antioch. From there they initiated a mission to the island of Cyprus by the Spirit's prompting, taking Mark along as their helper (Acts 12:25; 13:5). But when the group pressed ahead to the mainland of Pamphylia and arrived at the city of Perga, Mark's zeal for evangelistic work hit a wall. Rather than face danger with his fellow travelers, he sailed back to his mother's home in Jerusalem (Acts 13:13). Keep in mind that later on this trip, Paul was stoned and left for dead outside the city walls of Lystra (Acts 14:19). No wonder he resented the way Mark had chickened out! Paul wanted nothing more to do with such an unreliable partner. Yet Barnabas hoped to give his cousin a second chance. The book of Acts describes their dispute as follows:

> Now Barnabas wanted to take with them John called Mark. But Paul thought best not to take with them one who had withdrawn from them in Pamphylia and had not gone with them to the work. And there arose a sharp disagreement, so that they separated from each other. Barnabas took Mark with him and sailed away to Cyprus, but Paul chose Silas and departed, having been commended by the brothers to the grace of the Lord. (15:37–40)

Don't miss the seriousness of what has happened here. Mark's lack of faith not only resulted in personal failure—it created a split between two major church leaders!

Another Chance

We don't know how Barnabas's mission fared with Mark along, but what we do know is that Mark eventually found his way back into Paul's good graces. The events surrounding their falling-out took place around AD 46. Fast-forwarding by a decade and a half, we find the picture has changed for the better. Mark is no longer an unreliable partner in Paul's eyes.

It is now the early 60s, and Paul is under house arrest in Rome (Acts 28:16). He writes a letter to the Colossians in which he declares that Mark has been a true comfort to him (Col. 4:10–11). Around this same time Paul writes to Philemon and sends greetings from Mark, whom he describes as his "fellow worker" (Philem. 24). Then a few years after that, Paul writes to Timothy during a much more arduous imprisonment in Rome. Now he is desperate for Mark's presence. "Get Mark and bring him with you," he urges Timothy, "for he is very useful to me for ministry"

(2 Tim. 4:11). This is truly remarkable. The man whom Paul had refused to take on a missionary journey is now so useful for Christian service that the greatest apostle can't do without him!

So there it is: the wishy-washy Mark has pulled off a dramatic comeback. Though he failed at first, he seized the second chance God gave him and found a way to serve the church effectively. Even if he had accomplished nothing else, Paul's ringing endorsement would be enough to cement Mark's place in the annals of church history. Yet as we are about to see, the Lord had even greater things in store for this young man.

MINISTERING WITH PETER

Imagine having the opportunity to work alongside not just one but two great Christian leaders. Can you picture yourself proclaiming the gospel in Europe when Martin Luther was a veteran pastor and John Calvin was just getting started? Or striving to awaken the souls of colonial Americans alongside Jonathan Edwards and George Whitefield? Or sitting down with C. S. Lewis and J. R. R. Tolkien to hash out your own work of Christian literature? That must have been what it was like for John Mark. He wasn't just privileged to team up with the apostle Paul—he also worked with Peter.

We have already seen that back in the earliest days of the church, when Peter was still in Jerusalem preaching the newly risen Messiah, the first Christians used the home of Mark's mother, Mary, as their base of operations. It is not hard to imagine that the son of the house, a well-educated lad with budding spiritual interests, may have caught Peter's eye. Eventually Paul noticed him too, inviting him on the mission trip that—despite Mark's initial failure—would be the beginning of a lifelong ministry. Over the years, Mark would have remained in the apostolic inner circle. It should come as no surprise, then, that when Peter wrote a letter at the end of his life, he passed along greetings from someone he considered his dear "son": the very same Mark, now a middle-aged man, tested and proven in gospel ministry (1 Peter 5:13).

Peter's Influence on Mark's Gospel

But beyond this obviously warm relationship, do we have any evidence that Peter had shaped Mark's understanding of Jesus? In other words, is there any validity to the tradition that says Peter provided the content of Mark's gospel? As a matter of fact, there is.

The previous chapter introduced Papias of Hierapolis, an early church father who gathered information directly from the mouths of those who had interacted with the apostles. Papias describes his historical method like this:

> If, then, anyone came, who had been a follower of the elders, I questioned him in regard to the words of the elders—what Andrew or what Peter said, or what was said by Philip, or by Thomas, or by James, or by John, or by Matthew, or by any other of the disciples of the Lord. . . . For I did not think that what was to be gotten from the books would profit me as much as what came from the living and abiding voice. (NPNF2, vol. 1, C.H. 3.39.4)

What makes Papias's method so valuable is that it allows us to recapture some of the remembrances of the apostles themselves. Historians of classical antiquity would consider a source like this, which is close to the original events and displays a meticulous concern for accuracy, to be very reliable evidence indeed. Apparently Papias collected a great deal of apostolic information and recorded it in a five-volume work called *Expositions of the Oracles of the Lord*. Unfortunately, this work is now lost, so all we have are whatever excerpts the later church historian Eusebius decided to quote.

Peter's Interpreter

Among the things Papias recorded (and Eusebius passed along), we find this important recollection:

Mark, having become the interpreter of Peter, wrote down accurately, though not indeed in order, whatsoever [Peter] remembered of the things said or done by Christ. For [Mark] neither heard the Lord nor followed him, but afterward, as I said, he followed Peter, who adapted his teaching to the needs of his hearers, but with no intention of giving a connected account of the Lord's discourses, so that Mark committed no error while he thus wrote some things as [Peter] remembered them. For [Mark] was careful of one thing, not to omit any of the things which he had heard, and not to state any of them falsely.[1] (*C.H.* 3.39.15)

The prose here is complex, in English as well as in the original Greek. Let us analyze what is being said. First, we see that Mark is called Peter's "interpreter." The Greek word *hermeneutes* typically meant a person who served as a mediator between foreign languages. In other words, Mark was a translator.

The apostle Peter was originally a fisherman of modest education whose native tongue was Aramaic. Scholars debate whether he spoke any Greek. Probably he would have picked up a little of the language in his homeland of Galilee, but even if he didn't, his missionary work would have given him basic proficiency. Yet this is not the same as being able to write a polished document intended for wider circulation. Literacy was not easily obtained by small-town workingmen in the ancient world. Mark, however, was from a wealthy family (recall that he had a large house with servants). In the cosmopolitan city of Jerusalem, it is likely he would have been taught better Greek than someone could pick up from day-to-day usage. Therefore, it appears he was assigned to help Peter with literary tasks that were beyond the reach of a fisherman's basic language capabilities, such as writing letters or recording oral history. Mark served as Peter's translator from Aramaic into Greek as needed.

Taking Notes

The second thing we note from Papias is the method of Mark's literary activity. Unlike Matthew, Mark wasn't an apostle, so he couldn't record Jesus' actual words from memory. Instead he got his information from Peter. But recall that Peter was first and foremost a preacher. The kind of gospel message Peter proclaimed is exactly what we see in the early chapters of Acts: a declaration of the mighty deeds of Jesus the Messiah, interpreted in the context of Israel's Scriptures. As Papias pointed out, this task is altogether different than sitting down and composing a "connected account." Yet whenever the chance arose, Mark carefully copied the recollections of Peter about Jesus.

Take another look at the Papias quotation above. Twice it uses the word "remembered." The English translation is no more clear than the Greek when it comes to determining the subject of this verb, but it most likely refers to Peter. After all, Mark is declared not to have been a disciple of Christ, so he could not have "remembered" Him. Clearly it is only Peter who could have recalled the Lord's life with apostolic authority. Therefore Mark took down an accurate (though out-of-order) account of everything Peter remembered, committing no error as he recorded whatever the foremost of the disciples could bring to mind about his sojourn with Jesus on earth.

Think about what this would mean. Mark's satchel of pages—maybe even a single scroll or book—would now form an extremely valuable Christian document. Though it was a jumbled mess, it begged to be reshaped into a chronological narrative. With such a priceless resource in his possession, it is hard to imagine Mark *not* undertaking the editing job that so obviously needed to be done. And in fact, all the early church fathers after Papias agreed that he did. The attestation of Mark as the author of the gospel that bears his name is universal in the ancient church. For example, Irenaeus of Lyons confirms the remark of Papias when he states, "After [Peter's and Paul's] departure, Mark, the disciple and interpreter of Peter, did also hand down to us in writing what had been preached by Peter" (ANF, vol. 1, *A.H.* 3.1.1).

The second-century teacher in Alexandria named Clement stated, "As Peter had preached the Word publicly at Rome, and declared the gospel by the Spirit, many who were present requested that Mark, who had followed him for a long time and remembered his sayings, should write them out. And having composed the gospel, he gave it to those who had requested it" (NPNF2, vol. 1, *C.H.* 6.14.6).

Clement's successor at Alexandria, the brilliant scholar Origen, likewise had this to say: "The second [gospel] is by Mark, who composed it according to the instructions of Peter" (*C.H.* 6.25.5). These testimonies are corroborated by the fact that a third-century biblical manuscript, Papyrus 45, included Mark among its collection of the four gospels. What else needs to be said? There is very solid historical evidence that Mark wrote a gospel based on Peter's authority. Our only real questions are, when, where, and how did he do it?

MARK IN EGYPT?

As I mentioned in our book's introduction, the church historian Eusebius of Caesarea is an absolutely vital source for our knowledge of early Christianity. He wrote the bulk of his famous *Church History* sometime before AD 300. In that work he reports, "They say that . . . Mark was the first that was sent to Egypt, and that he proclaimed the gospel which he had written, and first established churches in Alexandria" (*C.H.* 2.16.1).

The Bishop of Alexandria

After Eusebius, several other church fathers also record Mark as the first bishop of Alexandria, and soon everyone believed it. Indeed this is still the view of the Coptic Church of Egypt today. Eventually a work called the *Acts of Mark* was composed to describe his youth, adult ministry, martyrdom, and burial in

Alexandria. Although the details of this writing are not likely to be accurate, scholars think it preserves elements from an earlier text called the *Martyrdom of Mark* that may provide legitimate evidence for a connection with Egypt.

Eusebius clearly was aware of church traditions that claimed a Markan foundation for the congregation at Alexandria, though it isn't clear what his sources were. He may have known a version of the *Martyrdom of Mark*, or he may be quoting from the writer Clement of Alexandria, whom he cites as the source for some of his information about Mark. Whatever their origin, the traditions Eusebius had received prove that some early Christians associated Mark with Egypt.

On the other hand, during the late third century when Eusebius was writing, the Alexandrian church had just begun to exert itself under the leadership of the noted bishop Dionysius. Only a few decades later, a decree from the Council of Nicaea named the three most eminent Christian congregations to be Rome, Antioch, and Alexandria (NPNF2, vol. 14, *First Ecumenical Council, Canon VI*). It is quite possible that in the course of the third century, the Alexandrian Christians were trying to enhance the standing of their church by establishing a connection to an original biblical figure as other prominent cities could do. This happened quite often in antiquity.

Yet why choose Mark? He wasn't an apostle, so his selection is somewhat strange if it was an outright fabrication. Why not choose one of the Twelve if you are making up a mythical founder? Furthermore, the Markan claim surely would have been questioned by the church fathers if it had no basis in reality. So perhaps there was an oral tradition of a visit by Mark to the city of Alexandria, and the story now blossomed to make him the "first bishop."

On Shaky Ground

The truth is, we know very little about Christianity in Alexandria for the first 150 years after the time of Christ. If Mark had visited there, the story could have survived in oral tradition until it became more widely recognized. Unfortunately, the oral tradition hypothesis is weakened by the fact that the Alexandrian writers Clement and Origen—both of whom comment widely on Christian affairs in their voluminous writings—make no special mention of Mark. The African writer Tertullian even went out of his way to list the cities and regions where he believed the various apostles had founded churches; yet he said nothing about Alexandria, the major metropolis of his own continent (ANF, vol. 3, *Prescription Against Heretics* 36). For these reasons, Mark's stay in Alexandria cannot be proven with absolute certainty. However, it is certainly plausible, and there are enough hints in the historical sources to think it may well have happened.[2]

A discussion of Mark's presence in Alexandria wouldn't be complete without mentioning one of the greatest hoaxes ever perpetrated in modern scholarship. In 1958, Professor Morton Smith of Columbia University discovered in a remote Greek Orthodox monastery what he claimed was a lost letter of Clement of Alexandria. In the letter, Clement quotes from a so-called *Secret Gospel of Mark*, which suggests homosexual behavior on the part of Jesus. Even if this letter really were from the hand of Clement, it wouldn't prove anything about the real Jesus, only that some second-century heretical sects believed scandalous things about the Lord (which Clement was trying to refute). Certain statements in the text also would have been the earliest evidence of Mark's presence in Alexandria. However, the supposed "secret gospel" has been debunked. Textual clues reveal it was actually forged by Morton Smith himself—including a clever allusion to his own name through a cryptic mention of salt![3]

Thus, there is no concrete evidence of a Markan connection to Egypt prior to Eusebius's testimony. While this ancient church historian does appear to have been relying on received traditions about Mark, we cannot be certain these accounts go back any earlier than the third century. Mark may have visited Alexandria, but we don't have early evidence for a long-term ministry there, much less for his martyrdom and burial—which means the stolen bones lying in Venice's San Marco cathedral probably belong to somebody else.

MARK IN ROME

So if Mark didn't write his gospel from Alexandria, what city was home to his scribal activity? The historical evidence most likely suggests he was based in the imperial capital. Not only do many church fathers connect him with Peter in Rome, the gospel itself suggests this when it uses Latin-based words as one would expect for a Roman audience (such as *kodrantes*, a Roman coin, in 12:42, or *centurion* in 15:39). Mark used Peter's preaching and memories as his story's foundation, though the shape of the present gospel indicates he also incorporated Jesus traditions from other sources. Rome was an early Christian focal point, so there would have been ample opportunity to collect firsthand stories about the Lord from many people.

Remember that Jesus had seventy-two disciples whom He sent on an evangelistic mission (Luke 10:1), as well as more than five hundred followers beyond that (1 Cor. 15:6). Some of these folks surely would have been available to Mark over the years, providing source material to round out what Peter could recall. This means Mark's gospel was more than just a rearrangement of Peter's sermons and stories. However, the transcription of the Petrine testimonies seems to have been the core of the work.

When did all this writing occur? Papias indicates Mark's note-taking took place during Peter's lifetime. Some scholars have understood Irenaeus's testimony (quoted above) to contradict this by suggesting Mark wrote *after* the deaths (i.e., the "departure") of Peter and Paul in the mid-60s, but this is a mistaken reading of the bishop's words. In context, Irenaeus was simply saying that Mark bequeathed a *written* gospel to later generations after the *living voice* of Peter and Paul had ceased—not that Mark necessarily composed it after their deaths. It seems, then, that in the years leading up to the early 60s, Mark served as Peter's translator and set about capturing a written record of the apostle's memories.

Colossians 4:10–11 and Philemon 24 prove that Mark was indeed in Rome at the same time as Peter and Paul. When it became apparent that the lives of these two eminent apostles were coming to an end, and that the living voice of the apostles was beginning to die out in the church, Mark composed a brief, vivid, and theologically distinctive gospel to serve as a fixed record for the second generation of Christians. Exactly when he did this is hard to say, but let us suggest a probable date of 60 or thereabouts. Then, recognizing the immense value of such a work, Christian messengers quickly took it to Antioch, where it was used by Matthew's community as we discussed in chapter 1. In our next chapter we will see that Luke also used it to construct his own version of the gospel of Jesus Christ.

☩

And so it was that the fainthearted Mark got a second chance—and did he ever make good use of it! He founded an entirely new literary genre: the Christian "gospel," a work of narrative, theology, biography, history, and evangelism all rolled into one. Other gospels soon followed, and it is hard to overestimate how influential they have been in world history. All this from a guy who once ran back to the safety of his home and left his fellow missionaries in the lurch. Not only did Mark overcome that failure to win Paul's favor again, he even ministered alongside Peter, the right-hand man of Christ Himself. Never mind the rags-to-riches stories of savvy businessmen or noted inventors. Mark the evangelist was the original comeback kid!

REPORT CARD

Collected and translated Peter's memories	A-
Wrote the gospel that bears his name	A
Wrote from Rome	A-
Was the first bishop of Alexandria	D
Visited or ministered in Alexandria	B
Is now buried in Venice	D

A= Excellent, B= Good, C= Average, D= Below average, F= Not passing

CHAPTER 3

LUKE

L oyalty. Faithfulness. Friendship that perseveres through hard times. Although these virtues are celebrated in history and literature, most of us would have to admit they're pretty hard to come by in real life. Think of those famous friendships like Sherlock Holmes and Dr. Watson. The Lone Ranger and Tonto. Batman and Robin. Captain Kirk and Spock. In each case, the loyalty of the sidekick helps the hero become a better man. Who wouldn't want a great friend like that? "A man of many companions may come to ruin," says Proverbs 18:24, "but there is a friend who sticks closer than a brother." If you have such a friend in your life, count yourself blessed.

The great apostle Paul had a faithful sidekick like that as well: Luke, a Gentile convert who accompanied Paul on his missionary journeys. Of course, the apostle had many traveling companions and coworkers during his lifetime of evangelism. Yet at the end of his life, when things had gotten risky for the Christians, it was Luke who stayed by Paul's side. One of the last sentences the apostle ever wrote testifies to this fact.

Imprisoned under harsh conditions and facing imminent death, Paul wrote mournfully about those who had opposed or deserted him. Just one man was left standing: "Luke alone is with me," Paul declared in 2 Timothy 4:11. After everyone else had run away, Luke remained.

This loyalty is depicted architecturally in the great church at Rome known as St. Paul Outside the Walls. All four corners of the church's lovely courtyard are empty save one. There, a statue of Luke holding a writing stylus commemorates not only his work as a gospel author but his faithfulness to Paul. Luke was truly a friend who stuck "closer than a brother."

A LOYAL FRIEND

Only a few facts can be deduced from Scripture about the life of Luke, since he is mentioned by name in a mere three verses. We have just seen how Paul referred to him as a faithful friend, even after Paul's other coworkers abandoned him in a Roman dungeon. Demas fled because he was "in love with this present world," while Crescens and Titus departed for perhaps more noble reasons (2 Tim. 4:10).

However, according to Colossians 4:14, both Demas and Luke had stood by Paul during his previous house arrest at Rome. In this verse we learn not only of Paul's fond affection for Luke but that he was a doctor by training—for Paul refers to him as "the beloved physician." At the same time that Paul wrote his epistle to the church at Colossae, he also penned a personal letter to his friend Philemon who lived in that city. Verse 24 again mentions both Demas and Luke as loyal coworkers. But only a few years later when Paul was facing death, it was Luke, not Demas, who proved himself faithful.

Travels with Paul

Though Luke is not mentioned by name anywhere else in Scripture, we can infer that he was one of Paul's traveling companions. As the narrative in the book of Acts unfolds, the unnamed author uses the first-person plural at certain points. He begins to say not just that Paul did such and such, but that "we" did various things, inserting himself into the narrative anonymously. Acts 16:10–17 describes how he joined Paul's evangelistic workers in AD 49 at Troas and went with them to Philippi. The author remained there while Paul continued on, but about eight years later he joined Paul's third missionary journey as the apostle passed through Philippi again.

From there the two friends eventually made their way to Jerusalem, arriving in the late spring of 57. Though it is not clear what the author did next because he stops using the pronoun "we," the detailed account in Acts 21–26 implies he was an eyewitness to the activities of Paul even if he was not a direct participant.

The Beloved Physician

For two years, Paul endured persecution and bore witness before the authorities in several trials. He was jailed for much of this time in the Roman port city of Caesarea. At last he was ordered to be transferred to Rome for trial before Caesar, departing in the late autumn of 59. It is at this point that the author of Acts resumes his first-person narrative (27:1–28:16). He describes the dangerous sea voyage—including the vivid details of a harrowing shipwreck—that finally brought the friends to the capital city. The author closes his story with the assertion that Paul remained under house arrest for two years, proclaiming the kingdom of God with boldness to all who would visit him.

Was Luke, the beloved physician mentioned in Scripture, the author of these "we" passages in Acts? The question must be considered in relation to the authorship of the gospel that bears his name. Most scholars today consider Luke and Acts to comprise a single two-volume work. Not only are both texts dedicated to a patron named Theophilus, the book of Acts also refers to an earlier volume that describes what Jesus said and did (Acts 1:1).

Furthermore, the same excellent Greek style unifies these two writings, and similar themes are addressed in both. The cumulative weight of the evidence suggests they were written by the same author. So again we may ask: Was this author Luke?

THE CHURCH'S MEMORIES OF LUKE

Church tradition universally attests that the biblical figure of Luke was the author of a canonical gospel, along with a second volume that came to be called the Acts of the Apostles. The earliest references to Luke's gospel are found in the church father Justin Martyr (mid–second century), though he does not cite Luke by name. But around the year 180, the noted bishop Irenaeus of Lyons makes the attribution clear. He writes, "Luke also, the companion of Paul, recorded in a book the gospel preached by [Paul]" (ANF, vol. 1, *A.H.* 3.1.1). A little later, Irenaeus asserts that Luke was "inseparable from Paul"; was his "fellow-laborer in the gospel"; and was "always attached to and inseparable from him." The "we" passages in Acts make this abundantly clear, according to Irenaeus. He says that Luke "performed the work of an evangelist, and was entrusted to hand down to us a gospel" (*A.H.* 3.14.1). Thus we can see that by the late second century, the early church had developed a tradition that these two works were the product of Luke's authorship.

Manuscript Evidence

Not long afterward, a manuscript of the gospel was copied by a scribe who attributed its composition to Luke. The surviving remnant of this manuscript is known today as Papyrus 75. It is a very early witness, not only to the gospel's Greek text but to the identity of the man whom the early church believed to have authored it.

Further textual evidence about Luke can be found in the prologues that were attached to several ancient biblical manuscripts by anonymous theologians. It is uncertain when these prologues

originated, but we should at least take note of the following assertions about Luke in the so-called Anti-Marcionite Prologue: (1)
he was a physician from Antioch in Syria; (2) he remained with
Paul until his martyrdom; (3) he had no wife or children; (4) he
died in the Greek city of Thebes at the age of eighty-four; (5) he
wrote his gospel after Matthew and Mark, intending it for Gentile
believers; (6) he afterward wrote Acts. Some of these claims will
be assessed in a moment, but for now let us note the clear attribution of Luke–Acts to the biblical figure of Luke, the traveling
companion of Paul.

Other Traditions about Luke

Following Bishop Irenaeus, the African church father Tertullian
also mentions Luke. In his work against the heretic Marcion,
Tertullian notes, "Of the apostles, therefore, John and Matthew
first instill faith into us; whilst of apostolic men, Luke and Mark
renew it afterwards" (ANF, vol. 3, *Against Marcion* 4.2). Tertullian's
point here is not the order in which the four gospels were written but that two had original disciples as authors, while the others were written by "apostolic men" who followed the disciples.
Tertullian goes on to state that just as Mark got his information
from Peter, so Luke's unique presentation of the gospel stems
from Paul.

A document called the Muratorian Fragment—a famous (though
somewhat inaccurate) discussion of which books should be in
the New Testament—likewise has some important things to say
about Luke. Scholars debate the exact time when this anonymous
canon list was written, with dates ranging from the late second to
the mid-fourth century. Personally, I believe the signs point to the
early end of the spectrum.

This poorly copied Latin text is very hard to translate, so I have
paraphrased what it says about Luke here: "The third book of the
Gospel is that according to Luke. The well-known physician Luke
wrote it in his own name, in proper order, after the ascension of

Christ, when he had become associated with Paul. Though Luke did not himself see the Lord in the flesh, he wrote his gospel as he was able, and began his narrative with the birth of John the Baptist" (see ANF, vol. 5, Caius, *Canon Muratorianus*). Again we see that by the end of the second century, Luke was widely considered to have authored a gospel.

Eusebius and Others

All (or at least most) of the above texts come from the period prior to the church historian Eusebius, who wrote his *Church History* around the turn of the third century. Eusebius sums up the tradition he had received when he declares,

> Luke, who was of Antiochian parentage and a physician by profession, and who was especially intimate with Paul and well-acquainted with the rest of the apostles, has left us, in two inspired books, proofs of that spiritual healing art which he learned from them. One of these books is the gospel, which he testifies that he wrote as those who were from the beginning eyewitnesses and ministers of the word delivered unto him, all of whom, as he says, he followed accurately from the first. The other book is the Acts of the Apostles, which he composed not from the accounts of others, but from what he had seen himself. And they say that Paul meant to refer to Luke's gospel wherever, as if speaking of some gospel of his own, he used the words, "according to my Gospel." (NPNF2, vol. 1, *C.H.* 3.4.7–8)

After Eusebius, the later church fathers such as Jerome and Epiphanius all agree about the authorship of Luke and Acts. This attribution was never disputed in the ancient church. No other candidate was ever put forward as the possible author of these works, whether in the writings of the church fathers or in any of the surviving biblical manuscripts. The tradition is unanimous: Luke, the beloved physician and friend of Paul, was the author of Luke–Acts. Our only question, then, is whether these ancient memories can withstand the scrutiny of historical investigation.

LUKE'S CONTRIBUTION TO THE NEW TESTAMENT

The gospel of Luke and the book of Acts together make up the largest section of the New Testament by a single writer—about 25 percent of the whole. If Luke was indeed the author of these works, he was privileged to have composed such a large part of sacred Scripture!

However, many scholars today reject the traditional claim that Luke wrote the two works attributed to him. At no point do the texts claim to be by Luke, and the theology of Acts is considered to be too different from what a true companion of Paul would have written. For example, Acts 16:3 portrays Paul as willing to circumcise Timothy in order to please the Jews, whereas in his own writings he adamantly resists circumcising Titus as an essential outworking of the gospel of grace (Gal. 2:3–5). Yet those who deny Lukan authorship must figure out a way to account for the presence of the "we" passages in the book of Acts. These scholars typically say that some anonymous author must have stitched together various sources—including a travel diary that used first-person language—without bothering to make any changes to the text he was excerpting.

But is this even remotely likely? The author of Luke–Acts shows far too much literary skill to make such a crude blunder as introducing an alien first-person narrator into the middle of his story. The normal reading of a first-person passage written by anyone with an ounce of editorial skill is to assume that the author is speaking about himself. Since we know Paul definitely had a fellow-worker named Luke (Philem. 24), and we also have the universal attestation of the early church that the gospel was written by this same man, the preponderance of evidence is on the side of Lukan authorship for the two-volume work of Luke–Acts.

Time of Writing

When exactly did Luke do his writing? Once again, scholars are divided. Those of a more liberal persuasion, who doubt Jesus could have foreseen the fall of Jerusalem to the Romans, claim the prophecy in Luke 21:20-24 is too accurate to have been predicted beforehand. It must have been written after the city's fall in AD 70. These scholars imagine that the anonymous author knew about the historic event and put words in Jesus' mouth to make it look as if He could predict the future. Therefore, "Luke's gospel" (written by an unknown person) must have been composed after the year 70. Then the book of Acts must have appeared at some later point.

But quite apart from the theological issue of whether Jesus could have made an accurate prophecy, there is a solid *historical* reason to date the book of Acts prior to 70: the way the text ends. Acts focuses especially on the story of Paul. It concludes with his two-year imprisonment in Rome, which lasted until 62—then nothing else is said about him. However, we know some very important events took place just a few years later.

In 64, a terrible fire swept through Rome, which Nero blamed on the Christians. Both Peter and Paul were martyred at this time (see chapters 9 and 10 for more about that). It is unthinkable that the meticulous historian who gave us such a detailed account of Stephen's martyrdom would omit what happened to his primary hero if he had known of it—especially after just telling his readers all about Paul's legal trials and perilous trip to the capital! Or, if Paul had been freed from house arrest to do further missionary work, perhaps even going all the way to Spain, it is highly unlikely that the writer whose motif was "the gospel's expansion to the uttermost parts of the earth" would fail to mention such events.

But perhaps Luke didn't include these things because he didn't know about them when he sat down to write his account. No, he certainly would have known. As we saw earlier, he was with Paul during his first imprisonment, and he was there five years later when Paul was in jail again. If Luke had written Acts after the events of 64–66, his manifest historical method leads us to the conclusion that he would have included such significant developments as the Great Fire of Rome, Nero's persecution, and two apostolic martyrdoms (or three if we include James's death, which happened at this time as well). These outcomes are extremely relevant to the overarching theme and narrative arc of Acts.

It is true that Acts climaxes with Paul reaching his goal of Rome—yet that is not a strong enough reason to think Luke would simply end the story with Paul under house arrest. If Luke knew what had happened to his key protagonists, the most reasonable conclusion is that he would finish the story. Ancient historians often included accounts of their heroes' noble deaths. For Luke to have this information at his disposal, yet fail to include it in his otherwise meticulous history, is not a sustainable hypothesis.

Therefore, Acts must have been written around AD 62, at the time Paul's house arrest ended. Since Acts 1:1 refers to an earlier volume, the gospel must have been composed a year or so prior to Acts. We need not imagine big chunks of time were needed to compose these works. Theophilus was probably a well-off Christian who financed Luke's historical studies as a full-time project. The writing of Luke–Acts could have been accomplished in a matter of months.

The Historian's Sources

Evidently Theophilus thought Mark's gospel—which many of the early Christians considered too abbreviated—required elaboration by a proficient Greek stylist like Luke. This new gospel, written by a Gentile historian with a pro-Pauline agenda, would nicely complement the previous effort of Mark. Yet Luke clearly valued Mark's summary of Peter's preaching, so he used it as the basic framework of his narrative. However, as he attests in Luke 1:1–4, he used other eyewitness recollections to round out his account. He could have obtained a version of the Q-source from the Antiochian community during the two years Paul was imprisoned at Caesarea (these two cities were not far from each other by sea), or perhaps he got it from James and the Jerusalem church during his visit there (Acts 21:17–18).

As for the other sources Luke may have used, it is impossible to say exactly what they were, so modern scholars simply designate them with the catchall name of "L." Together these three sources—Mark, Q, and L—provided the material that Luke used to compose his account of Jesus' life. And his own experiences, coupled with recent written and oral testimony, gave him what he needed for Acts.

So then, putting all the historical pieces together, it appears that Luke the physician wrote the second Christian gospel. He would have had access to Mark's gospel as soon as it was published, for the two men were together in Rome during the early 60s. The apostle Paul mentions them as being present with him during his first Roman imprisonment (Col. 4:10–14; Philem. 24). If Mark finished his gospel around 60, we can imagine that Luke—one of the few literate early Christians[1]—would have been immediately interested in the new text.

At this time Nero's persecution had not yet broken out, so the Christians could intermingle freely (Acts 28:30–31). Luke probably used the years during Paul's house arrest (that is, 60–62) to write his two-volume work with its steady focus on God's mission to the Gentiles. A little later, Mark's gospel made its way to Antioch. There, Matthew's school of Jewish-Christians refashioned Mark into the third New Testament gospel to be written (see chapter 1). Most of this editorial work occurred prior to 70, although a little adaptation of the Synoptic Gospels may have taken place later.

LUKE AFTER PAUL

So far, we have been reading between the lines of Scripture and sifting the memories of the church fathers to determine what Luke probably did in the final years of Paul's life. We have discovered that his major contributions were to remain faithful to Paul, and to compose a two-volume account of Jesus' life and the subsequent apostolic missions. But after Luke–Acts was published and Paul had been martyred, what happened to the beloved physician? Where did he go next, and where was he buried? The Bible is silent on these matters. Can church tradition fill in the gaps in our knowledge?

A little earlier we mentioned the text called the Anti-Marcionite Prologue to Luke, an ancient preface to the gospel that provided quite a bit of background information about Luke's later life. As always, the historian's first question is, when did this text originate? Scholars of a previous generation dated all the Anti-Marcionite Prologues to the late second century. More recent study has suggested that some of them may belong to a later time; but the notice about Luke is indeed early, which makes it much more reliable.

Luke's Death

Let us recall that the prologue places Luke's death in Greece—specifically in the city of Thebes. As it turns out, a little Greek Orthodox church nestled in a cemetery in modern Thiva (ancient Thebes) still contains an ancient marble tomb that claims to be Luke's. However, the lead coffin that once fit inside the tomb is no longer there. Why not?

The fourth-century church father Jerome tells us what happened to the original coffin and its bones. He recounts that Luke composed the book of Acts in Rome during Paul's two-year imprisonment. Jerome then declares that Luke "was buried at Constantinople, to which city, in the twentieth year of [Emperor] Constantius, his bones, together with the remains of Andrew the apostle, were transferred" (NPNF2, vol. 3, *Lives of Illustrious Men* 7). Other sources indicate a slightly different date for the transfer of Luke's and Andrew's relics to the Church of the Holy Apostles in Constantinople, but it is clear enough that this event did occur sometime in the fourth century. Then, several centuries later, danger and upheaval in that city prompted church officials to move the lead coffin of Luke again, this time to Padua, Italy, where it remains today. But did this coffin originally come from Thebes in Greece? And perhaps more interestingly—did it actually contain the very bones of Luke?

Old Bones

Here is where modern science enters the story. In 1992, the Greek Orthodox bishop of Thiva submitted a request to the Roman Catholic bishop of Padua that a bone from the lead coffin be sent to the original site of the tomb. The Catholic bishop was willing to help out, but first he wanted to do a detailed scientific analysis of what was inside the coffin. He enlisted a team of experts whose forensic work took several years.

The final results were astounding. The measurements of the lead coffin in Padua revealed it would fit exactly into the marble tomb at Thiva. Clearly the tomb and coffin were originally made for each other. When the coffin was opened, it was found to contain a single skeleton of a human male, about 5 ft. 4 in. tall, who had died after age seventy. The DNA analysis released in the prestigious journal *Proceedings of the National Academy of Sciences* (Nov. 2001) suggested this individual was likely to be of Syrian origin and had died between the years AD 72 and 416. Parallel marks from maggots on the skeleton and the coffin proved the body had decomposed in the container and had not been deposited there at a later time—in other words, the coffin's present skeleton was its original occupant. These discoveries were hailed as proof that the mortal remains were actually those of Luke.

Reliability Check

But not so fast. While the possible date range did include the time when Luke would have died (i.e., sometime after 72), the Italian scientist who conducted the study was quoted in the London *Daily Telegraph* and the *New York Times* as saying the most likely date for the individual's death was closer to the year 300. And according to an article in the Catholic journal *Traces*, ancient coins were found inside the coffin, the oldest of which was from 299. The shape of a cross incised on the side of the coffin also suggested a third-century date. At this period of history, many wealthier believers were seeking lavish church burials. This is just the time when we would expect an expensive lead coffin of a prominent Christian to be set into a marble tomb. However, the historical Luke probably died in the first century, when special ecclesial burials were not being given to Christians. We would therefore expect a less monumental grave for him.

It is certainly possible that Luke did go to the region of Thebes and die there. This would account for the oral tradition that developed in the ancient church. Based on this tradition, a third-century body in the local Christian cemetery came to be celebrated—whether by fraud or error is hard to say—as belonging to Luke. Around sixty years later, it was transferred to Constantinople, then Padua. Most of that skeleton remains in Italy today, though its skull was moved to Prague in the Middle Ages, and the rib closest to the saint's heart was donated to the bishop of Thiva for veneration in its original resting place. The sliver of bone can be seen today in a glass case next to the marble tomb. Although three different cities claim to possess the relics of Luke, unfortunately, the evidence suggests otherwise: the body and its coffin, which were originally interred together, appear to date to the third century. On the other hand, the DNA evidence does not absolutely rule out the possibility that the bones could have belonged to Luke.

Yet when all is said and done, what happened to the saint's body is beside the point. It's what Luke did during his lifetime that really matters. He was a man of intense loyalty, a friend who stayed at Paul's side through the good times and the bad. Because of his close relationships with the apostles and other eyewitnesses of the Lord, Luke was able to gather the pieces of a fascinating narrative and fashion them into a story that has been read by billions of people. Instead of missionary work or a heroic martyrdom, the 25 percent of the New Testament written by Luke is his true legacy for today.

REPORT CARD

LUKE		
Traveled with Paul on missionary journeys	A
Remained with Paul until the very end	A
Wrote Luke and Acts based on eyewitness sources and personal experiences	A-
Wrote his two volumes in the early 60s from Rome	B+
Used Mark as a source for his gospel	B
Went to the region of Thebes and died there	B-
Is now buried in Padua, Prague, and Thiva	D

A= Excellent, B= Good, C= Average, D= Below average, F= Not passing

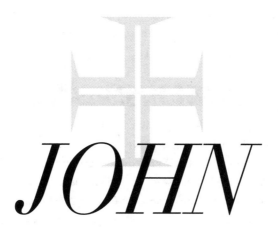

JOHN

The apostle John is such a worthy figure that his name has become one of the most commonly used in the Western world. Whether it is expressed as Juan in Hispanic regions, Ian in Britain, Jan in Scandinavia, Johann in Germany, Jean in France, Giovanni in Italy, or Ivan in Slavic lands—they are all forms of the famous apostle's name. It is no wonder that when we wish to mention a nameless person, we use the alias "John Doe" or "Jane Doe." Other feminized forms of the name include Janet, Jeanne, and Johanna.

All of these names trace back to the greatest John of all: the disciple of the Lord who is thought to have authored five biblical books. History has counted the apostle John worthy of remembrance.

Even so, John the son of Zebedee is something of an enigma in Scripture. While the Synoptic Gospels mention him frequently in conjunction with Peter, he remains unnamed in his own gospel. The book of Acts likewise gives him a little space at first, but he quickly drops off the scene as the narrative shifts to Paul. And what happens after that? Does John fade into oblivion? Not if you listen to the early church fathers. John is one of the few apostles who is believed to have lived to a ripe old age. This means several Christians of the second generation claimed to have interacted with him. In the case of John, it is especially true that church tradition rounds out the picture that Scripture presents.

THE MANY FACES OF JOHN

As we have already seen with the gospels of Matthew, Mark, and Luke, so with the fourth gospel we discover the early church was quick to assign an author to it. Ancient tradition agrees that the John who wrote this work was the Galilean fisherman who left his nets along with his brother James to follow Christ (Matt. 4:21–22). Later this same John was involved in the healing of a lame man (Acts 3) and was imprisoned with Peter (Acts 4). But after Acts 8:14, John disappears from the biblical record. Anything else we might wish to learn about him must be deduced from his writings, or from historical analysis of ancient church claims.

So did John actually write the fourth gospel as the early Christians record? And if so, when and from where? And what about his epistles, or the book of Revelation? Virtually all modern scholars from the liberal end of the biblical studies spectrum reject apostolic authorship for any of these books. Sometimes they say a different John wrote them and the early Christians became confused about his identity. Other scholars claim we simply cannot identify the author. In contrast, conservatives tend to be more willing to attribute most or all of the books to the apostle. Let us first address the authorship of these five texts before investigating the various traditions about what John did after he disappeared from the book of Acts.

The Unnamed Disciple

Not only does the fourth gospel never identify its author, it never even mentions the apostle John by name. There is, however, an anonymous figure who is referred to as the "other disciple"

(John 1:35–40; 18:15–16; 20:2–4) or the "beloved disciple" (John 13:23; 19:26; 20:2; 21:7; 21:20). Verse 24 of the book's final chapter identifies the beloved disciple as the author, a trustworthy eyewitness who knew the Lord well. Who could this mysterious person be if not the apostle John?

The other gospels depict John as one of the leading disciples, a member of Jesus' innermost circle along with Peter and James. He is mentioned twenty times in Matthew, Mark, and Luke. It is difficult to imagine how John could be completely absent from the narrative of the fourth gospel in such stark contrast to the other three. In light of this, the best hypothesis is that the gospel speaks about John, using cryptic third-person terms (perhaps out of humility, or because his editorial team referred to him that way, as discussed below). The fact that the beloved disciple reclined against Jesus at the Last Supper (13:23–25) makes it virtually certain he was one of the Lord's closest associates. This must have been John, since all the other disciples are otherwise named. Furthermore, the beloved disciple is almost always linked with Peter, which is exactly what we see in the Synoptic Gospels: Peter and John were Jesus' most intimate companions (e.g., Luke 22:8). Complex modern theories ought to give way to the obvious fact that John the son of Zebedee is the most plausible candidate to be the unnamed disciple mentioned in the fourth gospel.

The ancient church certainly believed this. Bishop Irenaeus of Lyons, writing around AD 180, declared that "John, the disciple of the Lord, who also had leaned upon his breast, did himself publish a gospel during his residence at Ephesus in Asia" (ANF, vol. 1, *A.H.* 3.1.1). From this statement it is clear not only that Irenaeus believed the apostle John wrote the gospel, but that this John was the unnamed "beloved disciple" who first appeared in the upper room reclining against Jesus' chest. Yet how could Irenaeus know this? Lyons is in France—a long way from Ephesus in Turkey! Could a bishop in ancient Gaul obtain accurate information all the way from Asia Minor? Absolutely. Irenaeus was one of many immigrants from Asia who had made their way to Gaul. As a boy,

Irenaeus sat at the feet of the leading Asian bishop Polycarp—a man who is said to have known John himself. The memory of Polycarp was burned into Irenaeus's mind. He recounts:

> I remember the events of [my boyhood] more clearly than those of recent years. For what boys learn, growing with their mind, becomes joined with it; so that I am able to describe the very place in which the blessed Polycarp sat as he discoursed, and his goings out and his comings in, and the manner of his life, and his physical appearance, and his discourses to the people, and the accounts which he gave of his intercourse with John and with the others who had seen the Lord.
>
> And as he remembered their words, and what he heard from them concerning the Lord, and concerning his miracles and his teaching, having received them from eyewitnesses of the "Word of Life," Polycarp related all things in harmony with the Scriptures. These things being told me by the mercy of God, I listened to them attentively, noting them down, not on paper, but in my heart. And continually, through God's grace, I recall them faithfully. (NPNF2, vol. 1, *C.H.* 5.20.6–7)

From this it is clear: Irenaeus had good authority behind his belief that John wrote the fourth gospel. He learned it from Polycarp, who knew John personally![1]

The Gospel Writer

After Irenaeus, all the church fathers agree—often independently of each other—that John wrote the fourth gospel. But is there any evidence that is substantially earlier than Irenaeus? In our previous chapter we mentioned the Anti-Marcionite Prologues, which were anonymous introductions attached to ancient gospel manuscripts to provide a little background for the reader. The Anti-Marcionite Prologue to John states that the gospel was published in Asia during John's own lifetime. Because this prologue is a much later work, it is not itself very reliable. Yet its quoted source for this information is the five-volume historical work by Papias of Hierapolis, who was writing at an earlier time. Papias is declared by the author of the prologue to have known the apostle well, and even to have been the scribe who took down John's dictation of the gospel.

While the dictation job might be a stretch, it's not entirely out of the question. Papias was born in the late first century and ministered in Hierapolis, which was only about a hundred miles from John's city of Ephesus. Thus, he was in the right place and time to serve the aged apostle as a scribal assistant. Bishop Irenaeus also attests Papias's personal acquaintance with John (ANF, vol. 1, *A.H.* 5.33.4). Since the Anti-Marcionite Prologue appears to have recorded an actual statement from Papias's lost five-volume work, it serves as further evidence that John himself wrote the gospel that bears his name.

A Complex Book

But if the evidence of John's authorship is so strong, why do virtually all liberal scholars today reject this idea? Their reasons for this conclusion cannot simply be dismissed as irreligious or overly critical. For the most part, their arguments stem from the astoundingly complex book that the gospel of John truly is. Within the text as we now have it, there are differences of Greek style; distinct sources of material; jumps, breaks, and scene changes in the narrative; inversions of chronological order; and repetitions of blocks of material. Chapter 21 also seems like an obvious appendix added later (see 20:30–31 for the end of the main narrative). All of this gives the distinct impression that the work was not penned by a single man at one time from personal memories but was a highly edited compilation that went through several stages of production.

The gospel is also known for its lofty philosophical thought. It hardly seems like the kind of thing a Galilean fisherman could produce on his own, even allowing for the development of his intellect and education over time. A fair reading of the gospel of John has to grapple with these realities.

John's Ghostwriters

Fortunately, a probable solution to this quandary is to be found in the ancient notion of authorship. Today we think of an author as a person who sits at a desk and writes a manuscript on a computer. The tools for doing this are widely available. According to this view of authorship, the editor only enters the process to suggest revisions or touch up minor errors in the manuscript. But consider John—a decent Greek speaker, though by no means an expert in the second language he had picked up along the way. A true literary education was hard to come by in the ancient world. John wouldn't necessarily have felt comfortable publishing a work intended for native Greek speakers. And let us also remember that the highly refined skills of handwriting and textual production would not have been part of his background. In light of this, John would have needed helpers to assist him in publishing a text.

Just as we saw with Matthew in Antioch, so we can imagine that a small circle of educated believers in Asia Minor took responsibility for John's final literary output. Such notions of authorship weren't at odds with the ancient way of thinking about literature. To be an "author" meant a person caused a book to be written under his "authority." It didn't require the author to think up every word or write them all down himself, only to ensure that his personal voice was properly represented. A scribal team was a normal part of the process; cooperation was the name of the game. Books were rare and precious, so if you were fortunate enough to possess sources of any kind, you freely incorporated them into your own work. As long as the ostensible author gave the impetus for the final manuscript to be composed and published, the work could circulate under his name even if it didn't reflect his individual writing style.

In the case of the fourth gospel, we seem to have a book that is at once a group effort and John's own work. That would have satisfied the ancient audience for whom it was intended, even if it now contradicts our pious image of an aged apostle with a pen in his hand. John's recollections as an intimate friend of the Savior provided the vital substance of the fourth gospel. It is truly "his" gospel, for he shared his own memories with his scribal associates and directed their writing. The authority of John stands behind the work.

Nevertheless, the text as we now have it reflects some editorial freedom in stitching together various sources and oral traditions and personal testimonies. There is no reason the Holy Spirit could not have inspired this process just as He preserved the apostle's own memories. John 21:24 makes this cooperative effort obvious. After declaring that the beloved disciple was the one "bearing witness about these things, and who has written these things," the verse goes on to add, "and *we know* that his testimony is true." Who is this outside "we" here? Clearly it was John's editorial community affirming that he was an accurate source and worthy author of the gospel.

When Was the Gospel Written?

If John the apostle did indeed publish his gospel with the help of others, when did this occur? It is impossible to be precise, but we have good reason to think the task was finished by around AD 100. The earliest existing piece of a Greek New Testament manuscript is a little scrap called Papyrus 52 that preserves a portion of John 18. This manuscript is dated by scholars to the early decades of the second century. But the papyrus fragment was discovered in a remote part of Egypt. We would expect some time to have elapsed between the original writing in Ephesus and its arrival in a fringe community by a process of hand-to-hand transmission.

Thus we are pushed back to around 100 for the gospel's final form. This squares with the testimony of Irenaeus, who claimed the apostle John survived into the reign of Emperor Trajan from 98–117 (ANF, vol. 1, *A.H.* 2.22.5). Interestingly, this dating could also fit with the suggestion that Papias served as John's scribe.

A time frame like this would have to presume John was quite young, possibly even a teenager, when he was following Christ (which explains why he outran the middle-aged Peter to arrive first at the empty tomb in John 20:4). If John was nineteen at the time of the resurrection, he would have been in his eighties when his gospel was finally completed. We can suggest it achieved final form around 95 to 100, though only after several years—maybe even decades—of editorial work by John's literate helpers.

THREE LETTERS

In our Bibles today we also have three letters traditionally ascribed to John. Technically, the first is anonymous, while the second two are attributed to a figure who calls himself the "Presbyter" (meaning "elder"). Scholars believe the letters bear a strong affinity in Greek style and theme to the fourth gospel, so they probably had the same author, or at least were produced by the same literary community. But the question here is whether the "Presbyter" was the apostle John. The debate centers around a certain statement made by Papias—a very unclear remark that convinced not only the ancient historian Eusebius but also many modern scholars that there were two distinct "Johns" in this discussion. Papias said:

> If, then, any one came, who had been a follower of the elders [*presbyters*], I questioned him in regard to the words of the elders [*presbyters*]—what Andrew or what Peter said, or what was said by Philip, or by Thomas, or by James, or by John, or by Matthew, or by any other of the disciples of the Lord, and what things Aristion and the *presbyter* John,

the disciples of the Lord, say. (NPNF2, vol. 1, *C.H.* 3.39.4, emphasis added)

Eusebius, who recorded this remark of Papias, suggests it proves the existence of two Johns—the disciple and the presbyter. However, take a closer look at what is being said here. Papias is not distinguishing two Johns; he is contrasting the disciples who are dead with those still alive. Most of the disciples are described with a past-tense verb. Though they "said" certain things about Jesus, they no longer speak with a living voice. However, two long-lived disciples, John and the unknown figure named Aristion, could still "say" things about the Lord.[2]

The disciples of Jesus are consistently called "presbyters" in this text, so there is no good reason to create a "John the Presbyter" distinct from the apostle. The word *presbyter* was simply Papias's term for an apostle in this passage. Why? He was probably just reflecting the language of 2 and 3 John, where the author identifies himself by this word (v. 1). Therefore, the three Johannine epistles are attributable to the one-and-only John, the apostle of Jesus Christ—though again, the editorial work of John's team of helpers is apparent in these texts.

END-TIMES PROPHECY

The book of Revelation is also ascribed by tradition to the apostle John, but here we stand on a little shakier ground. Clearly a figure who identifies himself as "John" wrote it (1:1), but who was he? Scholars take varying views on the authorship question. Though it is generally understood that Revelation has a Johannine tone, it is nonetheless distinct in its Greek style, theology, and worldview when compared to the gospel or the three letters. This may indicate that the editorial method of John's helpers differed from that of the other Johannine texts. Yet that does not mean the nucleus of the text, including the original vision granted to the author, cannot stem from the apostle John himself.

One reason Revelation bears such notable thematic and stylistic divergence from the letters and the gospel might be that it was the earliest text to enter into an editorial process within the Johannine school. There is good reason to think the original vision was first recorded in the year AD 68, after which time several hands may have helped Revelation achieve its final form under the Spirit's guidance. Why 68? For one thing, emperor worship appears to serve as the background to the text, and the province of Asia was very much a center of this cult in the 60s—a trend that was only going to intensify in the years ahead.

But even more specific is the assertion in Revelation 13:17–18 that 666 is the "name of the beast." Many commentators have noted that when the numbers are converted to Semitic letters, they spell the words "Nero Caesar." Note also the reference in Revelation 17:9–11 to seven mountains (clearly a reference to Rome's famous seven hills) and eight kings—five of whom have already fallen, while the sixth currently exists, the seventh will come soon, and the eighth will be a terrible beast from out of the seven, who is headed for destruction. Late in the year 68, five Roman emperors had already died: Augustus, Tiberius, Caligula, Claudius, and Nero. Emperor Galba was in power, but Vespasian was making plans to supplant him, and widespread rumors at the time (not just among Christians but even the wider population) expected a revived Nero to return from the dead—the eighth king from out of the seven, according to John. All of this points to a date just after the reign of Nero. However, some church fathers attest a later date for the composition of Revelation during the reign of Emperor Domitian (AD 81–96). This may reflect the end of the editorial process that gave us the book as we now have it.

All in all, then, we have good reason to connect John the apostle with the five biblical books attributed to him, especially his gospel and the three letters. Yet we can also see that John was the leader of an interpretive community that helped shape his final literary output.

JOHN, BISHOP OF EPHESUS?

So far we have seen that John's primary legacy to the church after the ascension of Christ was to serve as a New Testament author. Along the way in our study, we have noted that Ephesus was considered the traditional location for John's later life. Some church traditions even attest he died as a martyr. To close out our examination of John, let us take a look at these claims.

As noted above, Irenaeus of Lyons tells us John wrote from Ephesus. Irenaeus even recalls a funny story he received from Polycarp: that one day John encountered the arch-heretic Cerinthus at the bathhouse in Ephesus, so he fled the scene with the cry, "Let us fly, lest even the bathhouse fall down, because Cerinthus, the enemy of the truth, is within!" (ANF, vol. 1, *A.H.* 3.3.4).

The attestation of John's Ephesian residence is supported by Irenaeus's contemporary Polycrates, the bishop of Ephesus, who says that John "was both a witness and a teacher, who reclined upon the bosom of the Lord, and, being a priest, wore the sacerdotal plate. He fell asleep at Ephesus" (NPNF2, vol. 1, *C.H.* 5.24.2–3). Though the notion that John was a Jewish priest stems from a confusion with the John mentioned in Acts 4:6, we can still see that in the late second century, the bishop of Ephesus was making the claim that John had lived and died in his city.

The claim is likewise made by Justin Martyr, who resided for a time in Ephesus (ANF, vol. 1, *Dialogue with Trypho* 81). There is really no solid reason to dispute the tradition on this point. The Johannine writings are widely understood by scholars to arise from the region of Asia in which Ephesus was the leading metropolis. The island of Patmos where John received his revelation is just off the Ephesian coastline. It seems likely, then, that church tradition is correct in claiming the apostle John went to this great city and became the leader of all the nearby Christian communities. (The interesting question of whether John took Mary the Lord's mother with him to Ephesus will be addressed in our next chapter.)

JOHN'S DEATH

A few scattered accounts suggest that John died violently as a martyr, but these sources all come from a time when martyr stories were blossoming everywhere, so they have to be considered suspect.[3] Probably they were attempts to expand on Jesus' assertion in Mark 10:39 that John would drink the cup of the Lord's suffering. For this reason a noble death had to be invented for John.

In contrast, the church father Tertullian records the story of John being immersed in boiling oil and emerging unscathed. It was at Rome, Tertullian writes, that "the Apostle John was first plunged, unhurt, into boiling oil, and thence remitted to his island-exile" on Patmos (ANF, vol. 3, *Prescription Against Heretics* 36). Today the alleged spot of John's boiling at Rome is marked with a chapel called San Giovanni in Oleo, but this story is quite a stretch.

Similar legends were being penned at the same time about Peter and Paul because the early church had a voracious appetite for heroic fiction about their founding figures. This is why the second- or third-century source known as the *Acts of John* was written (ANF, vol. 8). Although its story of John's death, in which the apostle lays down in a grave dug by his assistants and calmly expires, is acknowledged to be legendary, the text once again attests a widespread Ephesian tradition for John's residence in his later life. The earliest and best evidence leans toward a long life for John, not a martydom.

Modern visitors to Turkey can visit the apostolic grave at the ruins of the Basilica of St. John in Selçuk, which is near the ancient site of Ephesus. The church whose ruins are visible today was built by the Byzantine emperor Justinian in the sixth century on top of an earlier chapel from around AD 400. This Byzantine church was once magnificent, with eleven domes on its roof, intricate mosaics on its floors, and a spacious courtyard out front. But did it cover the actual grave of John? Second-century coins were found in the tomb, indicating it may have been a place of Christian veneration quite early. The hillside location is attested as a Roman cemetery.

However, there is no firm evidence John's actual body now lies there, or that it ever truly did.

✠

Yet perhaps it is fitting that the apostle who was first to reach the empty tomb of Christ is likewise missing a well-established grave—for Christianity is not about the bones of the dead but eternal life in the Risen One. Of all people, the man who recorded the Savior's words "I am the resurrection and the life" (John 11:25) surely understood this. It was an eternal truth that changed everything for this fisherman from Galilee, launching him on a lifelong mission that took him far from his boyhood home. But John didn't shrink back from the demands placed upon him. The young disciple who had once leaned on the bosom of Jesus knew that after a life of Christian faithfulness, he would once again sit in intimate fellowship with his Lord. Indeed, it was John who wrote that anyone who opens the door to Jesus will dine with the Son of Man, and whoever overcomes the world will share His heavenly throne (Rev. 3:20–21). Surely this is a promise that will inspire "beloved disciples" in every generation.

REPORT CARD

JOHN

Wrote the five Johannine biblical books by himself	C
Is the substantial author of the fourth gospel	A
Is the substantial author of the three epistles	A
Is the substantial author of Revelation	B+
Lived in Ephesus	A
Died as a martyr	D
Is buried in the ruined basilica at Ephesus	C-

A= Excellent, B= Good, C= Average, D= Below average, F= Not passing

CHAPTER 5

MARY

A few years ago, a strange phenomenon appeared on my daily
commute along the Eisenhower Expressway in Chicago.
Precipitation runoff and road salt leaching from the concrete
wall of an underpass had created a stain that vaguely resembled
a veiled woman. The stain was considered by some local residents to be an apparition of the Virgin Mary. Flowers and candles
were placed at the foot of the stain, and soon graffiti made its
appearance as well, both appreciative and hostile. I found myself
astounded by all the religious attention awarded to something as
inconsequential as a blotch on a highway wall. Although I was
aware of popular Internet rumors in which the Madonna was said
to have appeared in a potato chip or a grilled cheese sandwich,
this was my first encounter with such superstitious devotion up
close. It all seemed so primitive. I quickly dismissed the Marian
nonsense from my mind.

✠

But is that the right response? Is Roman Catholic devotion to the
Blessed Virgin Mary so outlandish that we can safely ignore Mary
altogether? Or does this form of spirituality have legitimate roots

in the ancient church, and perhaps even in Scripture? Those who are turned off by modern veneration of the Blessed Virgin must not forget that the angel Gabriel declared Mary the "favored one" of God (Luke 1:28), and the historical evidence indicates she was a very important figure in the earliest church. It is therefore worth asking, who was this woman? And what do we know of her life after her Son ascended back to heaven?

EARLY LEGENDS OF MARY

The early Christians loved to hear pious stories about their founding figures. It wasn't long before legends and tales celebrating the apostles' deeds began to circulate throughout the church, and Mary the mother of the Lord was no exception when it came to starring in fictional narratives. One of the most important documents to arise in the ancient period was a biography of Mary supposedly written by her other famous son, the apostle James. This so-called *Proto-Gospel of James* was actually composed by an unknown author in the last half of the second century, yet it struck a chord, and soon Christians everywhere accepted its stories as true. Though the *Proto-Gospel* later came to be doubted by leaders in the Western church, its outline of Mary's biography would go on to have a long life in popular piety and medieval religious art.

Proto-Gospel of James

The *Proto-Gospel* begins with the account of a rich Jew named Joachim and his wife, Anna, who could not bear children. Deeply saddened by their barrenness, the couple cried out to the Lord. At last when Anna heard from an angel that she would conceive, she promised the child would be dedicated to temple service (much like the prophet Samuel in the Old Testament). In time, Anna gave birth to a baby girl. When young Mary was three years old, her parents took her to the Jerusalem temple, where she was accepted by the priests and the people with great joy. Mary was nurtured like "a dove that dwelt there, and she received food from the hand of an angel" (ANF, vol. 8, *Protevangelium of James* 8).

But when Mary turned twelve (and presumably was about to begin menstruating), the priests grew concerned she might defile the temple. Therefore an elderly widower named Joseph was chosen by a miraculous sign to be Mary's husband, though only as a paternal caretaker so her virginity would be retained. The years passed until one day, while sixteen-year-old Mary was weaving a veil for the temple, an angel appeared with the message that the Son of the Most High would be born to her, even though she was a virgin. Mary accepted the responsibility and soon her belly began to grow. But when Joseph discovered it, he was distraught and planned to divorce her secretly. Weeping bitterly, Mary proclaimed her innocence, and an angel confirmed her story to Joseph. However, the temple priests did not believe the couple's testimony until the "water of the ordeal of the Lord" was administered (Num. 5:11–30). This test proved the couple was telling the truth.

At last the day of Mary's delivery arrived. She and Joseph were traveling to Bethlehem for the Roman census when the baby began to come forth. After turning aside and leaving Mary in a cave, Joseph ran to find a Hebrew midwife. At first the midwife doubted the story of virginal conception, but when she saw the miraculous light in the cave as Jesus was being born, she believed. Yet her friend Salome, another midwife, would not believe until, like Doubting Thomas, she extended her finger and tested that Mary's hymen was still intact. Salome's unbelief caused her hand to burn like fire until she repented and worshiped the baby Jesus in her arms, which healed her. The narrative then concludes with the visit of the wise men, King Herod's slaughter of the innocent Jewish children, and the martyrdom of Zacharias, the father of John the Baptist.

Faith Worthy of Honor

How much of this story is historical? An honest scholarly appraisal would have to conclude: very little. Its content appears out of nowhere, disconnected from a reliable stream of Marian information, and with certain anachronistic touches that signal it is from a later time.

The real value of the narrative stems not from what it tells us about the actual Mary, but from how it displays the fond affection that the early Christians felt for this virginal girl. Long before Mary received any grand titles such as "Queen of Heaven" or "Mother of the Church," she was a devout young Jew who, when confronted with the incredibly daunting prospect of giving birth to the Messiah, replied, "Let it be to me according to your word" (Luke 1:38).

Though the *Proto-Gospel of James* is legendary, it celebrates Mary on much the same basis as the Bible does—for her holiness, courage, purity, and faith. The earliest traditions treat Mary as an example of piety, not a mediator of divine grace.

DEVOTION TO MARY GROWS

Over time, the ancient Christians' devotion to the Blessed Virgin Mary began to expand. A complete history is impossible here, but perhaps a few key points can be noted. Mary was first discussed theologically by the church fathers in the context of Christ's actual human birth, contradicting the Gnostic view that Christ wasn't a true man. Ignatius, the second-century bishop of Antioch, argues for a properly balanced Christology by referring to the Savior as "both of flesh and spirit; both made and not made; God existing in flesh; true life in death; both of Mary and of God" (ANF, vol. 1, *Epistle to the Ephesians* 7). Warning against the lies of the heretics, Ignatius advises, "Stop your ears, therefore, when any one speaks to you at variance with Jesus Christ, who was descended from David, and was also of Mary; who was truly born, and did eat and drink" (*Epistle to the Trallians* 9). For the earliest church fathers, Jesus' birth from His mother, Mary, was proof of His true humanity. The Son of God had become a man.

Comparison to Eve

The Blessed Virgin was also treated by some ancient writers as a parallel to Eve. Just as Adam fell into sin but Christ undid his evil work (1 Cor. 15:21-22), so the Savior who was "born of a woman" (Gal. 4:4) canceled the divine curse upon the woman (Gen. 3:15). Picking up on this woman/woman parallelism, Irenaeus of Lyons wrote, "As the human race fell into bondage to death by means of a virgin [Eve], so is it rescued by a virgin [Mary]; virginal disobedience having been balanced in the opposite scale by virginal obedience" (ANF, vol. 1, *A.H.* 5.19.1). In other words, when Mary accepted the angel's assignment for her, she counterbalanced Eve's original refusal of God's commandment to abstain from the fruit. Typologies like this, in which Old Testament events point ahead to New Testament fulfillment, were very common among the ancient church fathers.

Tales of Perpetual Virginity

By the third century, Mary was also being widely venerated for her lifelong chastity and permanent refusal of sexual relations. As the tide of asceticism began to rise within the church, she was increasingly hailed as an icon of sexual purity. Though we have already seen that the *Proto-Gospel of James* went to great lengths to demonstrate—even to the point of supplying medical evidence!— that Mary remained a virgin up to the time she gave birth, the conclusion that she continued to renounce sex for the remainder of her lifetime now became widespread among third-century Christians, especially through the influence of ascetically minded writers like Origen (see ANF, vol. 9, *Commentary on Matthew* 10.17).

By the fourth century, Mary had begun to receive the theological title *aeiparthenos*, Greek for "ever-virgin." However, this belief had more to do with the celebration of monastic virtue that was so common at the time than with the likely experience of the Jewish bride whom the carpenter Joseph married. He clearly kept Mary a virgin until she gave birth to Jesus (Matt. 1:25), but the "until" in this verse implies Joseph had sexual relations with his wife afterward—which is, of course, something the Bible celebrates (Gen. 2:24).

Nevertheless, Christian tradition from the third century until contemporary times has argued for the perpetual virginity of Mary. Jesus' brothers mentioned in Scripture are interpreted either as cousins, or as sons of the widowed Joseph from his previous marriage (on this point, see the discussion of James in chapter 7). Today, the Roman Catholic and Eastern Orthodox churches maintain that Mary remained celibate her entire life, while most Protestants do not feel the need to make that claim.[1]

THE CULT OF THE BLESSED VIRGIN

A true "cult of the Virgin"—by "cult" we mean a widespread religious system with prayers, liturgies, architecture, and formal theology, not necessarily a heretical sect—began to arise in the late fourth century, and blossomed especially in the fifth. Saints of the church were highly respected in the 300s, and Mary was certainly prominent among them; but it was the Council of Ephesus in 431 that really made devotion to her skyrocket.

The issue at this council was how to explain the deity and humanity of Jesus Christ. When did the Savior become divine—at His conception, or at some later point when the man named Jesus was infused with divine power? The correct theological answer is that Jesus of Nazareth has been divine from the moment He was conceived. He is the eternal Son of God who became incarnate within a woman's womb. One way of expressing this truth is to call Mary the "Mother of God" (*Theotokos* in Greek). In other words, she did not give birth to a mere man whom God adopted as His Son at a later time. Rather, the baby within Mary's uterus was fully divine from the point of conception. Through miraculous means, a human mother gave birth to God Himself.

Often in my church history class, I surprise my students by declaring to them, "We evangelical Christians must affirm the vital doctrine that Mary is the *Theotokos*, or Mother of God!" For the next several days, my students think I am some kind of closet Roman Catholic, at least when it comes to my views of the Blessed Virgin. However, I always clear it up later by explaining that what I said was actually a *Christological* point: Mary was the mother of God the Son[2] from the moment the Holy Spirit overshadowed her and gave her conception (Luke 1:35). That is why the bishops at Ephesus in 431 called Mary the "Mother of God": to affirm Christ's full deity from the very beginning of the incarnation (NPNF2, vol. 14, *Anathematism I*). Therefore, it is entirely appropriate to refer to Mary with this title, as long as the Christological meaning is made clear.

Unfortunately, the affirmation of Mary as the *Theotokos* in 431 had the unintended effect of galvanizing the church's affection for her and propelling it to new heights. Indeed, the grand Ephesian cathedral where the council took place—remodeled from what was once a monumental Roman meeting hall—was already devoted to Mary. Though its crumbling remains can be seen today by modern visitors to Ephesus, back in late antiquity it was certainly no ruin. The cathedral was a thriving center of devotion to the Virgin, nearly one-and-a-half football fields in length.

Several other Marian churches soon sprang up after the council, including three in the imperial capital of Constantinople, as well as a very important one in Rome called Santa Maria Maggiore. While this Roman church has now lost its ancient appearance due to later decorations, it is still a stunning piece of architecture. Those who wander close to its altar will encounter fragments of wood that purport to be from the manger of baby Jesus. Over the centuries, many more churches and cathedrals have been devoted to Mary, such as Notre Dame and Chartres Cathedral in France, the Duomo in Milan, and the Basilica of Our Lady of Guadalupe in Mexico City.

LATER MARIOLOGY

Observers of contemporary Christianity will know that certain doctrines about Mary are widely cherished by the Catholic faithful. We have already seen that her perpetual virginity and the designation "Mother of God" have roots in ancient times, though not explicitly in the New Testament itself. But other Marian doctrines are much more recent. For example, the belief in Mary's sinless birth, known as her immaculate conception, only became official Catholic dogma in 1854. Likewise, the bodily assumption of Mary directly into heaven at the end of her life was declared to be true based on the infallible statement of Pope Pius XII in 1950.

The assumption is also taught by the Eastern Orthodox Church, though under the name of her "dormition," which refers to Mary's death followed by a speedy resurrection straight into God's presence. While some late ancient and medieval documents do suggest this idea (see discussion below), it was not taught by the Christians of the first four centuries.

All of these doctrinal pronouncements seem to have led us very far from the Jewish girl whose Hebrew name was Miriam of Nazareth—the real girl who was confronted by a glorious angel and gave a resounding yes to her divine mission. When we peel back the many layers of church tradition, what actual truths can be affirmed about the historical figure whom we know today as Mary?

MARY AFTER JESUS

Outside of the birth narratives in the early chapters of Matthew and Luke, Mary plays a limited role in the pages of Scripture. She seeks the boy Jesus in the temple (Luke 2:41–52), interacts with Jesus when He turns water into wine at Cana (John 2:1–12), and gathers with the apostles in the upper room when the Holy Spirit descends (Acts 1:14).

But the most significant text for our present purposes is John 19:25–27, for it is the only New Testament passage that may hint at what became of Mary after her biblical story ends.

While hanging on the cross, Jesus addressed His beloved disciple and His mother, who were standing nearby. "Woman, behold, your son!" Jesus exclaimed to Mary, then turned to the beloved disciple and cried, "Behold, your mother!" At this point, the text of John's gospel offers a parenthetical comment about what happened after the moment of the crucifixion: "And from that hour the disciple took her to his own home." We saw in chapter 4 that the beloved disciple was probably the apostle John. We also saw how a community of his followers in the region around Ephesus helped to edit his gospel into its final form. Did these editors include the side note about Mary's later life because they knew she had come to Ephesus under John's safekeeping? Or were they simply aware of John's care for her at some other location?

Mary in Ephesus?

A few church traditions do in fact connect Mary with Ephesus. Around AD 377, the intrepid heresy-hunter Epiphanius of Salamis published a refutation of eighty groups he considered unorthodox. Responding to the scandalous notion that unmarried men and women might cohabit under the same roof, Epiphanius mentions the case of John and Mary. He claims that although John "received" Mary to himself, she didn't necessarily "stay at his side" for the remainder of her life. The Scriptures are, in fact, completely silent about Mary's final years.

"And although John embarked on a journey throughout Asia," Epiphanius remarks, "nowhere is it stated that he brought the holy Virgin with him" (*Panarion* 78.11.2). Though Epiphanius did not accept the tradition of Mary's Ephesian residence, his comment suggests that some other Christians in the late fourth century did believe she had dwelled there. This would explain why the cathedral where the Council of Ephesus took place a few decades later was dedicated to the Mother of God.

One of the leading participants at the council, Cyril of Alexandria, stated in a letter that the city was associated with both Mary and John. And it is no coincidence that Ephesus would be receptive to the Blessed Virgin, since it had long been the site of a temple to Artemis, an ancient goddess who was also a virgin mother.

Certain features of that worship were readily transferable to a new female religious figure. Intense devotion to Mary was therefore a natural fit in this city.

Yet the belief that Mary resided at Ephesus was by no means widespread in ancient times. Other than the few hints mentioned above, we really don't see this idea stated plainly until the 800s. The association grew stronger over the years, until eventually it became firmly entrenched in popular Christian imagination.

Then in the early 1800s, the tradition seemed to receive striking confirmation when a German nun named Anne Catherine Emmerich experienced mystical visions instructing her where to find the "House of the Virgin Mary." Today this building at Ephesus has become a major Marian site for the Catholic faithful. Several recent popes have even made pilgrimages there. I recall visiting the place with my students a few years ago. We encountered a nun from Lourdes whose enthusiasm for Mary would have matched the zeal of the most ardent street evangelist. Although the Roman Catholic Church does not take a firm stance on the validity of the house, this has not prevented swarms of Christian pilgrims (and Muslims, who also venerate Mary) from flocking there.

Rethinking Mary in Ephesus

Chronology, however, presents a problem for the question of Mary's residence at Ephesus. Let's do the math. The probable date for the birth of Jesus Christ is 5 BC. Given that Jewish girls typically married in their early teens, we can estimate Mary was fifteen when she became a mother, which gives her a birth date of 20 BC. But John probably didn't go to Ephesus until the mid-60s AD. Otherwise, why would the apostle Paul, who spent three years there in the 50s (Acts 20:31) and wrote to the Ephesians in the early 60s, never mention John, a prominent disciple of the Lord?

In the previous chapter, we placed John in the vicinity of Ephesus when he received his Patmos vision of 68. Probably, then, he would have arrived in Ephesus a few years earlier, around 65 (which explains Paul's silence about John). But that would make Mary eighty-five years old at the time of John's arrival—quite an advanced age for a woman to take such a rigorous journey. In fact, only a tiny fraction of Greco-Roman women ever reached the age of eighty, and by then, these fortunate survivors would have been at death's door. Therefore, a better hypothesis is that Mary remained in Jerusalem for many years under John's care, just as the Lord had commanded. Her eventual death in the mid-60s freed the apostle to depart for evangelistic work in Asia.

As it turns out, some ancient church documents do contradict the Ephesian tradition by making the Holy Land the location of Mary's death (or bodily assumption). The genre of Marian biographies exploded in the fifth century, and it is only in this era that we find widespread discussion of the assumption or dormition of the Blessed Virgin. These texts consistently situate Mary in Jerusalem or Bethlehem, not Ephesus. For example, both *The Book of John Concerning the Falling Asleep of Mary* and *The Passing of Mary* describe how John was snatched up from Ephesus and deposited in Jerusalem so he could be with Mary as she was about to die (ANF, vol. 8). Today there is even a "Tomb of Mary" next to the garden of Gethsemane—which is not occupied by any mortal remains, of course, since Mary passed directly into heaven after resting in the tomb for three days. Only her sash was left behind as proof to Doubting Thomas that she had really ascended. Once again, these legends do not tell us much about the actual Mary, except to establish the primitive memory that she lived out her final years in Jerusalem. This appears to be more likely than an Ephesian residence.

AN ENDURING LEGACY

Miriam of Nazareth was a young Jewish girl whose purity and faith pleased God. "Greetings, O favored one," the angel said to her. "The Lord is with you!" It is a truly remarkable greeting. What was running through Mary's mind when she was told the

Most High God would overshadow her and conceive a baby in her womb? We will never be able to grasp such a mystery on this side of eternity.

Yet thanks to Mary's humble submission to her call, the Lord of the universe became incarnate within her body and was delivered in a lowly stable. The Blessed Virgin Mary, as she came to be known to Christians, is rightly honored for her role in this divine drama. She was cherished by the first believers as the chosen instrument of God.

Yet over time, this honor expanded until it was allowed to get out of hand as speculative theologies and pious backstories were invented to meet the demands of popular religion. Even so, the exaggerations of ancient and medieval Marian devotion shouldn't cause us to set aside this heroine of faith. Though we know little about her life after the biblical record ends, we should still consider her worthy of the title "Blessed Virgin Mary." As she herself exclaimed in one of the most beautiful prayers ever recorded, "My soul magnifies the Lord, and my spirit rejoices in God my Savior, for he has looked on the humble estate of his servant. For behold, from now on *all generations will call me blessed*" (Luke 1:46–49).

Christians of every type, from ancient times until now, owe an eternal debt of gratitude to this young woman for what she agreed to do. In Mary's willingness to become the vessel of the incarnation, she has modeled for all believers the right response to the often fearsome call of God. "Behold, I am the servant of the Lord," she said. "Let it be to me according to your word" (Luke 1:38). May every Christian have the courage to say the same in their moment of divine vocation.

REPORT CARD

MARY

Was cared for by John during her later life	A-
Was revered by the early church	A
Went to Ephesus with John	D
Dwelt in the "House of the Virgin" in Ephesus	F
Died in the Jerusalem area	B+
Maintained perpetual virginity	D-
Was bodily assumed into heaven	F

A= Excellent, B= Good, C= Average, D= Below average, F= Not passing

CHAPTER 6

THOMAS

In the city of Rome, not far from the pope's cathedral, lies the Basilica di Santa Croce in Gerusalemme, that is, the Basilica of the Holy Cross in Jerusalem. This church began as a remodeled chapel inside the imperial palace of Helena, the pious mother of Emperor Constantine. Helena has gone down in history for her attempt to recover precious relics of the Christian faith. After making a pilgrimage to Palestine, she is said to have brought back important physical remains and placed them in her palace chapel. At some point, soil from the Holy Land was even spread on the floor so the sacred mementos could be said to rest "in Jerusalem."

The modern visitor to the basilica will also discover a more recent chapel built in the twentieth century—the Chapel of the Holy Relics. Here the visitor will find (dubiously, it must be admitted) the following items on display: some fragments of the True Cross; the transverse beam from the cross of the good thief; a portion of the sign that hung above Jesus' head at the crucifixion; two briers from His crown of thorns; and one of the nails that pierced His body. Yet perhaps the most arresting sight of all can be glimpsed inside an ornate silver reliquary. It is the crooked finger bone of a human skeleton—the very finger that was placed into the Savior's wounds by the apostle Thomas himself.

THE APOSTLE'S UNFORTUNATE NICKNAME

As this macabre display illustrates, Thomas has been remembered through the ages for his one moment of stubborn unbelief. "Unless I see in his hands the mark of the nails," he declared, "and place my finger into the mark of the nails, and place my hand into his side, I will never believe" (John 20:25). No matter that Thomas later uttered one of the most important biblical confessions of Christ's deity when he exclaimed, "My Lord and my God!" (John 20:28), or that he had been willing to meet death with his Master (11:16). The unfortunate apostle will always be known as "Doubting Thomas." Throughout art history—whether on an ancient Roman coffin, a Byzantine icon, or a Renaissance altarpiece—the image of Thomas probing the wounds of Christ has served to highlight his wavering faith. Caravaggio's renowned painting *The Incredulity of Saint Thomas* (1602) portrays the examination of the Lord's gashed side with such astonishing intimacy and gritty realism that Thomas seems to be performing a crude autopsy.

But is the disciple's doubt the only thing about him worth remembering? Though his grand failure has been immortalized in the literary and artistic tradition, the ancient Christians had several other points they wanted to make about Thomas—recollections of a more positive sort that tend to be forgotten today.

JESUS HAD A TWIN?

The name Thomas comes from the Aramaic word for "twin." The gospel of John, which was written in Greek, likewise identifies Thomas as *Didymus*, or the Twin (11:16; 20:24; 21:2). Apparently, Thomas had a twin brother, yet the identity of this individual is nowhere stated in Scripture. Could it have been Jesus? Nothing in the New Testament suggests it, yet the possibility was irresistible to later generations.

By the late second or early third century, two separate texts, the *Acts of Thomas* and *The Book of Thomas the Contender*, had both put this claim into writing. The notion of Jesus' twin brother caught the attention of certain mystics who were interested in alternative perspectives on the Son of God. Though orthodox Christians sometimes read the *Acts of Thomas* for its inspirational value, this document was even more cherished among the heretical sects. Likewise, *Thomas the Contender* is full of Gnostic motifs. The identification of Thomas as Jesus' twin caused him to be viewed as a revealer of knowledge to a chosen few. The Gnostics quickly adopted Thomas as one of their favorite disciples. How come?

In today's world of modern medicine and safe childbirth, parents typically rejoice when they learn they are having twins (once they get over the shock!). But in many underdeveloped nations, twins are associated with a higher degree of infant mortality and complications in delivery. The second-born child of the pair, if it survives, also tends to be smaller and weaker. This was true in the times of the Roman Empire as well. The emergence of a second child after the first one caught the parents by surprise and didn't bode well for the family. According to the ancient mindset, the second child was a mysterious double, a shadowy person who wasn't supposed to be there. The "real" child got the family name, while the unexpected interloper was given a generic name like Thomas. Twins were always suspicious, unlucky, a bad omen.

Yet in the case of the apostle Thomas, his secondary status as a twin was offset by his being the supposed brother of Christ. Thomas was therefore an enigmatic figure—at once close to Christ and yet unlike Him. To certain ancient sectarians, he seemed like an insider who might know Jesus' private teachings, yet be willing to betray his brother's secrets. Thomas was the man in the know, the man beckoning you from the inner circle, the man who might whisper secrets if you could only learn how to ask.

In other words, to some observers, Thomas looked like the perfect Gnostic.

The Gospel of Thomas

It was perhaps inevitable that Thomas the Twin would come to be considered the author of a gospel. Who better to tell the story of Jesus than His own brother? Yet any reader of the so-called *Gospel of Thomas* will see it is notably different from the four gospels of the New Testament. Though it contains some cryptic remarks that are reminiscent of verses in Matthew, Mark, or Luke, the *Gospel of Thomas* is nothing but a collection of wisdom sayings. An overarching narrative structure—including the story of Christ's death and resurrection—is entirely lacking.

Instead, Jesus presents 114 distinct maxims that include tidbits such as, "When you strip without being ashamed, and you take your clothes and put them under your feet like little children and trample them, then you will see the son of the living one and you will not be afraid," or, "The Father's kingdom is like a person who wanted to kill someone powerful. While still at home he drew his sword and thrust it into the wall to find out whether his hand would go in. Then he killed the powerful one."[1] This work's obvious lack of sound theology made it a marginal text in the ancient church. Though its origins and intended uses are obscure, what we do know is that it eventually came to be endorsed by the Gnostic sects, but it wasn't cherished enough by the church fathers to be regarded as sacred Scripture.

Even so, that hasn't stopped many modern scholars from trumpeting the *Gospel of Thomas* as one of the most important documents of the "early Christians."[2] The claim is often made that this gospel is equal in value to the four canonical gospels in the Bible, and even contains true sayings of Jesus that are not found in Scripture. This historical hypothesis rests on the assumption that scholars can discern layers within the existing document that come from an earlier time; in other words, some experts claim to discern segments of the text that were composed before the canonical gospels were written. These bits supposedly reveal Jesus as a mystical philosopher, not a Jewish prophet who was about to usher in the kingdom of God on earth. The Jesus depicted in this gospel saves people by calling them to find truth within themselves and to ascend as immaterial spirits to a kingdom of light, not by dying for their sins and rising from the dead to give new life.

Yet this interpretation of Jesus is questionable because it cuts against the grain of the existing historical evidence. The lone surviving manuscript of the complete *Gospel of Thomas* was discovered in 1945 among a cache of Egyptian documents called the Nag Hammadi Library. Although the papyrus containing *Thomas* was physically copied in the fourth century, most scholars agree the text itself was probably authored in the second. The question is: Do certain editorial layers of the text go back to an earlier time, revealing a Jesus of spiritual enlightenment instead of a coming King and risen Lord?

The Real Status of the *Gospel of Thomas*

Unfortunately for those who want this to be true, all of the earliest sources that speak about Jesus' teaching—Mark, the sayings collection called Q, and the independent sources used by Matthew and Luke—portray Him as having taught an imminent kingdom within the context of Jewish hopes and expectations. Likewise, the earliest Christian proclamation about Jesus (recorded as creedal formulas and preaching within the New Testament) confessed that He was the Lord and Christ whose kingdom would soon arrive now that He had risen from the dead.

In contrast to this perspective, the Gnostic type of belief system found (at least partially) in *Thomas*, in which mankind needs to be awakened to secret truths, is only securely attested in the second century and beyond. That is why the trend among more reliable scholars today is to interpret Jesus as a prophet of first-century Palestinian Judaism, not as a teacher of inner enlightenment.

When good historical methods are applied to the *Gospel of Thomas* instead of subjective literary rereadings, the text settles into place as exactly what it appears to be: a cryptic composition from the second century that has excerpted and reworked pieces of the biblical gospels in a way that the Gnostics found appealing. By interspersing these borrowed Bible verses with a hefty dose of mystical imagination, then undergirding it all with the authority of Jesus' supposed twin, an anonymous writer has produced a philosophical Savior who bears little resemblance to the actual carpenter from Galilee. According to this Jesus, humanity's problem is lack of self-awareness, and the solution is wise interpretation of various precepts and parables. Fortunately, the four biblical gospels give us a more accurate picture of the Lord Jesus Christ.

Infancy Gospel of Thomas

Before we turn our attention away from fanciful speculations and back to the actual work of Thomas, we ought to debunk one more gospel that supposedly came from his pen. Some ancient writers who admired Jesus imagined His twin brother would be a great source of stories about what the Savior did as a little boy. Very little is said about Jesus' youth in the Bible, so the urge to fill in the gaps was strong.

To meet this need, several unknown authors claimed Thomas's name and constructed a set of narratives that are commonly called the *Infancy Gospel of Thomas*. This text regales us with such marvelous stories as the boy Jesus using His powers to slay His accursed playmates; to make clay sparrows fly; to resurrect a boy who died after falling from a roof; and to magically stretch wooden beams to repair Joseph's carpentry errors (ANF, vol. 8, *G.T.: First Greek Form*). All of these fables downplay the historical figure of Jesus and present Him as a divine prodigy. This theological tendency is a hallmark of the heretics.

Just as we saw with the *Gospel of Thomas*, the *Infancy Gospel* has absolutely nothing to do with the actual disciple whose name was borrowed as the presumed author. Although the association with Thomas may have been enough to cause orthodox Christians to read these texts on occasion, for the most part they were used by sectarian groups. How, then, did the mainstream church tend to remember Thomas?

THOMAS AND THE CHURCH IN INDIA

The Assyrian Church

A quick glance at a Bible atlas or a map of Paul's missionary journeys will give the distinct impression that Christianity's expansion from Jerusalem was only a westward trek. That notion is entirely mistaken. Although the other half of the story isn't as well known, the early Christian movement also expanded eastward into Persia, India, and China, where it thrived for a thousand years before being severely diminished by persecution. Only a small remnant of this church has survived today: the Assyrian Church of the East, sometimes called the "Nestorian Church." This Christian communion is *not* a type of Roman Catholicism or Eastern Orthodoxy. It is a distinct branch of Christianity that traces itself back to the Jerusalem church of Acts—and it does so especially by appealing to the missionary work of the apostle Thomas.

Acts of Thomas

Our earliest source of historical information about Thomas comes from a document we mentioned above, the third-century *Acts of the Holy Apostle Thomas* (ANF, vol. 8). It is a problematic text because it is full of dubious legends, legalistic morality, and questionable doctrine. Even so, because it presents one of the original apostles as a heroic miracle worker and successful evangelist in faraway lands, some orthodox Christians valued it, or at least were familiar with its contents.

The story opens with the disciples casting lots to determine who should evangelize which country. Though the job of going to India falls to Thomas, he refuses because the trip is hard and the foreign land is filled with Gentiles. Yet Jesus isn't going to give up so easily. He sells His twin brother, Thomas, as a slave to an Indian merchant looking for a carpenter to build a palace for his king.

Upon arriving in India, Thomas finds the people impoverished and suffering. Instead of using King Gundaphoros's funds to build the palace, he distributes all the money to the poor. The king, of course, is furious when he learns of the betrayal, but Thomas informs him about the heavenly palace that awaits the convert to Christ. Unimpressed with this future hope, King Gundaphoros resolves to execute Thomas. However, when the king's brother dies and returns from heaven, he informs Gundaphoros that a palace really does await him. Now the royal family and local populace convert to Christianity, which becomes a catalyst for Thomas's further evangelistic adventures and miraculous deeds in India.

At last, after great success among the Indian people, the apostle is martyred by a wicked king named Misdeus. Thomas is taken to a mountaintop, where the soldiers spear him to death. But then Misdeus discovers his son is demon-possessed, so he opens Thomas's tomb to find a bone that will drive away the unclean spirit. Although an unknown Christian has already removed Thomas's relics back to the west, some dust from the tomb serves to exorcise the prince. Misdeus repents and believes in Christ, proving that Thomas is an evangelist even after death.

Edessa

Since the *Acts of Thomas* is so full of legends, the historical background of its composition will tell us more about the apostle than any of the fanciful details we find recorded in the text. The earliest surviving version of *Acts of Thomas* is preserved neither in Greek nor Latin but in Syriac—an ancient form of the Aramaic language that Jesus Himself spoke.

Most scholars associate this document with the great city of Edessa (modern Urfa, Turkey), a prominent intellectual center of

Syriac-speaking Christianity. One legend even says King Abgar V of Edessa received a letter from Jesus promising that a messenger would come with the gospel; and sure enough, Thomas made good on the promise and sent a disciple to Abgar, who accepted the Christian faith (NPNF2, vol. 1, *C.H.* 1.13; and see chapter 8 for more on this myth). Edessa wasn't far from the biblical city of Antioch—less than two hundred miles along a good Roman road, and certainly reachable from the Holy Land. Thomas could have gone there quite easily. Many other Christians did. The people of Edessa may well have preserved an ancient memory of an apostolic visit.

But the metropolis of Edessa was just one of the many great cities within the original heartland of the Assyrian Church of the East. Today that region lies within the national borders of Syria, Turkey, Iraq, Iran, and even Afghanistan. Although these are now Islamic countries, the Christian church that once flourished there has preserved a deep awareness of its apostolic roots.

The ancient testimony was universal across this region that Thomas established the Church of the East (aided by the apostles Thaddeus and Bartholomew, as we will see in chapter 8). Because of the widespread literary and archaeological records attesting to Thomas's connection with the lands east of Jerusalem, the claim that he took the Christian message in that direction seems more likely than any other hypothesis. So the real question is: How far east did Thomas go?

The Thomas Christians of India: North

Two traditions describe the presence of Thomas in India. Generally speaking, we may characterize them as northern and southern. The *Acts of Thomas* represents the northern perspective because the foreign kingdom that Thomas visits in the story actually was ruled by a real king named Gundaphoros IV (alternately spelled Gondophares). Many ancient coins attest that a succession of kings with this name reigned in the first century AD, which is when Thomas would have been evangelizing the kingdom. Today this region is located in northwestern India, Pakistan, and Afghanistan, but in ancient times it was part of the Parthian Empire.

The fourth-century church historian Eusebius passes along the views of earlier Christians when he asserts, "The holy apostles and disciples of our Savior were dispersed throughout the world. Parthia, according to tradition, was allotted to Thomas as his field of labor" (NPNF2, vol. 1, *C.H.* 3.1.1). This Indo-Parthian kingdom was definitely accessible to the Romans. The network of overland trade routes called the Silk Road connected northern India with Rome, and so did a sea route linking the mouths of the Indus and Euphrates Rivers (the latter of which was the Roman Empire's easternmost frontier). Therefore, the northern evidence suggests that if Thomas did reach "India," it would have been the territory of the Indo-Parthian ruler Gundaphoros IV. This region later established close contacts with the Syriac-speaking Christians of Edessa.

The Thomas Christians of India: South

On the other hand, some very old traditions link Thomas to the southern tip of India along the Malabar Coast in the present state of Kerala. This area was also in contact with the Roman Empire by a sailing route that went to Egypt. The problem with accepting the historical validity of these southern accounts, however, is that they are primarily oral folklore passed down through generations of Christians, now recorded in sacred songs. Because these tales describe Thomas constructing a royal palace and being martyred by a spear thrust, many scholars believe the songs are later adaptations of the *Acts of Thomas* with local details added.

Even so, they likely preserve the primeval memory that Christianity had gained an early foothold along the Malabar Coast. Long-standing genealogies among priestly families, along with carved stone crosses from the early medieval period, serve to corroborate the great antiquity of Indian Christianity. The apostle Thomas is thought to have arrived at the great port of

Muziris, which once served as a stop along a thriving international trade route with the Roman Empire. Ships could sail from Muziris up the Red Sea to ports in Roman Egypt and back again, so it would have been entirely possible for a first-century Jew to travel from Jerusalem to Alexandria, and from there to reach India's southwestern coast in a matter of weeks. Today the various Indian churches that call themselves "Saint Thomas Christians" fiercely defend the apostolic founding of their communities in the Malabar region.

Thomas in India Examined

So did Thomas go to India or not—and if so, to which part? Here we can only speak of probabilities, not certainties. Christianity appears to have existed in Kerala by at least the second century. Eusebius says a second-century missionary named Pantaenus went to India from Egypt and found believers there (NPNF2, vol. 1, *C.H.* 5.10.3; see also Jerome, NPNF2, vol. 3, *Lives of Illustrious Men* 36). On the other hand, the tradition that Thomas himself went to southern India is based on flimsy evidence passed down by word of mouth.

And even the northern tradition is questionable. The *Acts of Thomas* could easily be a fictional account written at Edessa to elevate the famous apostle of the Assyrian Church. A scholar from Edessa named Bardaisan had recently compiled a history of India that might have provided a few of the historically accurate details found in the *Acts*. Since the text closely parallels other ancient fiction about the apostles, we are right to view it with a skeptical eye. The most we can say is that Thomas's evangelistic journey to India was (a) widely attested among the ancient sources, and (b) physically possible along established trade routes. Yet from the perspective of a critical historian, there is no solid evidence during the first 150 years after Thomas's lifetime to prove he went to India.

THE DEATH OF THOMAS

The tradition of Thomas's martyrdom has come to be associated with a little hillock called St. Thomas Mount in modern Chennai on India's east coast. Though the ancient accounts do tell us that Thomas died in India by spearing, the suggestion that it happened at Chennai is the stuff of pious fabrication. Only in the medieval sources do we begin to see a connection between Thomas and the eastern side of India. The sixteenth-century Portuguese explorers who sought to convert the indigenous Indian Christians to Roman Catholicism are responsible for the hilltop shrine at Chennai and its supposed bone fragment from the apostle.

The earlier and more reliable accounts suggest Thomas died in a different part of India, then his relics were moved in the third century from India to the Syrian capital of Edessa. In fact, the original composition of the *Acts of Thomas* may have been prompted by the establishment of such an eminent apostolic tomb in that city. This holy place soon became celebrated among Christians. For example, the liturgical poet Ephrem the Syrian wrote a hymn in the mid-fourth century describing how Thomas's "hallowed bones" defeated the devil and caused him to wail, "The apostle whom I slew in India is before me in Edessa!" (NPNF2, vol. 13, *Hymn XLII.1*).

A few decades later, a Spanish nun named Egeria (or Etheria) described her pilgrimage to Edessa to pray at the same apostolic shrine that Ephrem had celebrated. "We arrived at Edessa in the Name of Christ our God," she recalls, "and on our arrival, we straightway repaired to the church and memorial of saint Thomas. . . . The church there is very great, very beautiful and of new construction, well worthy to be the house of God." According to Egeria, "at the memorial of S. Thomas the Apostle . . . his body is laid entire."[3] All of this confirms the ancient association of Thomas with Edessa and the Assyrian Church of the East.

During the Middle Ages, however, Edessa was conquered by the Crusaders from western Europe. In the upheaval of those days, the sacred bones of Thomas were moved to the Greek island of Chios, then to Ortona, Italy, where they have remained since 1258. Today the Basilica di San Tommaso at Ortona possesses a crypt that claims to house the relics of the apostle.

But of course, the most important part of that holy skeleton has made its way to Rome: the actual finger that probed the wounds of Christ—or so it is said. As you can probably discern by now, the contradictory nature of the ancient traditions, as well as the intercontinental transport of Thomas's relics, make it unlikely the bones in Santa Croce are actually his. But does that even matter? The real Thomas wouldn't have wanted us to gaze on his dead finger but to look where his finger was pointing: at his Lord and God, the living Jesus Christ.

Although Thomas did experience a moment of doubt, he didn't remain locked in unbelief. According to the best evidence we have, his encounter with the risen Christ launched him on an evangelistic mission to faraway lands in the east. It must have taken a lot of faith to leave the security of home and travel to the end of the world with a message that might result in death. Perhaps history's most famous doubter would better be known as Daring Thomas!

REPORT CARD

THOMAS

Was the twin brother of Jesus	F
Wrote Gnostic gospels about Jesus	F
Went eastward to Edessa	A-
Went to northern India	B-
Went to southern India	C-
Died in India as a martyr	C-
Died on St. Thomas Mount (Chennai)	F
Was eventually buried at Edessa	A-
Has a finger bone on display in Rome	D

A= Excellent, B= Good, C= Average, D= Below average, F= Not passing

CHAPTER 7

JAMES

While working on my PhD in religious studies at the University of Virginia, I soon realized the locals held Thomas Jefferson in high esteem. Everyone referred to him as "Mr. Jefferson," as though he were going to come strolling across the university grounds at any moment. Though all my professors held doctorates, they had to be addressed as "Mr." or "Mrs." instead of "Dr.," lest anyone arrogantly presume to outshine the university's founder.

Yet as popular as Thomas Jefferson is around UVa, his identity as a forward-thinking educator is just one of his many personas. He can also be viewed as one of our country's greatest statesmen; or a typical Virginia gentleman at home on a farm; or an inquisitive scientist and inventor. Less positively, some contemporary historians have focused upon his ownership of slaves in the context of colonial America. Each of these personas could be the basis of a Jeffersonian biography. Apparently there isn't just one Thomas Jefferson. Many different claimants vie for his legacy.

WHO WAS JAMES?

The same is true for the biblical figure of James, the brother of the Lord. The ancient Christians and heretics alike tried to make James their own. Drawing from whatever traditions they had received about him, various groups constructed the persona for James that they found most appealing. And it didn't help that there were several "Jameses" to work with in the New Testament.

The Hebrew name for James, *Ya'akov*, was common among Jews of the first century. Although the present book is primarily interested in what happened to the apostles after Acts, when it comes to James we first have to discern his identity within the pages of Scripture. So let's try to grasp James as he appears in the Bible, then see if we can discover which of the later traditions about him have the greatest claims to authenticity.

Five Jameses

There are three clearly distinguished Jameses in the New Testament, plus two others who are less well known. Scholars both ancient and modern have held different theories about how to match them all up.

First, there is James the son of Zebedee. He and his brother, the apostle John, were called "sons of thunder" by Jesus (Mark 3:17). This James, often referred to as James the Great, will be discussed in our next chapter.

The second James is another one of Jesus' disciples and was the son of Alphaeus (Mark 3:18). He is usually called James the Less for reasons that will become clear in a moment. This figure will likewise be mentioned in the next chapter.

The third James is the man we are focusing on in the present chapter—the brother of the Lord. Typically he is called James the Just to distinguish him from James the Great or James the Less. These, then, are the three main Jameses of the New Testament.

But now things get interesting. In Mark 15:40 we hear of yet another James described as *mikros*, that is, the littler, younger, or lesser one. This is the source of the nickname James the Less. Early church tradition has often equated this James with the son of Alphaeus, combining them into one figure. However, they might actually be distinct, which means the man noted in Mark 15:40 would be a fourth James.

To complicate things further, several church fathers such as Jerome and Augustine equated James the Less of Mark 15:40 not only with James the son of Alphaeus but also with James the Just, the brother of the Lord. Now perhaps you are asking yourself, "How could the son of Alphaeus be Jesus' brother? Wouldn't he have to be the son of Joseph and Mary instead?" That is exactly right. The interpretation I'm describing here is the Roman Catholic view.

This reading suggests the word "brother" in ancient Jewish thought could have included cousins as well. Therefore, the James whom Scripture identifies as the "brother of the Lord" (Matt. 13:55; Gal. 1:19) was actually Jesus' cousin, so he could have Alphaeus as his father. As noted in chapter 5, once the doctrine of Mary's perpetual virginity developed in the ancient church, Jesus' brothers had to be explained away. Some church fathers attempted to do so by equating James the Just with the son of Alphaeus, who is presumed to be Jesus' uncle. Roman Catholics today believe James the son of Alphaeus = James the Less of Mark 15:40 = James the Just, the "brother" (but actually the cousin) of Jesus. This one man is distinct from James the Great, the brother of the apostle John.

Though I hesitate to say it, there is actually a fifth James in the New Testament. (This is really complicated, I know, but stay with me.) He is the father of the disciple Judas/Thaddeus, mentioned in Luke 6:16 and Acts 1:13. Fortunately, we don't know anything else about this James, so that's all we need to say about him.

Where does this leave us? Roman Catholic interpreters, relying on early church writers who were trying to avoid assigning Jesus any literal brothers, collapse three Jameses into one (as noted above), and distinguish him from two others. On the other hand, the Protestant view that I and many other scholars hold is that the

New Testament mentions four or five separate Jameses. Although it is possible that the son of Alphaeus is also the man mentioned in Mark 15:40, we should probably view all five Jameses as distinct: the Great, or son of Zebedee; the son of Alphaeus; the Less of Mark 15:40; the brother of Jesus; and the unknown father of the disciple Judas (not Iscariot).

Whew! What a tangle! This has certainly been a complex discussion. However, we needed to clarify which biblical James is the focus of the present chapter. He is the firstborn son of Joseph by his wife, Mary, which makes him the brother (or technically, the half brother) of Jesus, whose mother was also Mary.

What else can we learn from Scripture about this James? It was he who played such a crucial role in determining the place of the Jewish law in the Christian faith at the Jerusalem council of Acts 15. This James is also the traditional author of the epistle that bears his name. But did he write anything else? If the ancient Gnostics are to be believed, he produced a lot more than just one letter in the New Testament. In fact, an entirely new persona for James emerges among the Gnostics. Let us turn our attention now to the figure of James in postbiblical tradition.

THREE APPROACHES TO JAMES

James the Gnostic?

The set of beliefs that goes by the name "Gnosticism" has been difficult for scholars to define (see the introduction). But even when we admit that Gnostic teaching was variable and complex, and that it sometimes overlapped with things the orthodox church fathers believed, this religious and philosophical movement is distinct enough from the message of the earliest Christians that it ought to have a separate designation. The central idea of Gnosticism is that revelation of secret knowledge helps humanity escape the evil physical world. Therefore, the twin emphases of *gnosis* (knowledge) and *askesis* (bodily self-discipline) are commonly found among the Gnostics.

This is where James comes in. As we saw with Thomas, so also with James, his status as the Lord's brother made him an excellent candidate for secret revelations. Likewise, the traditions that describe James as an ascetic who disciplined his body for spiritual purposes also made him appealing to the Gnostics. The sectarian groups found excellent basis for their exalted view of James in the *Gospel of Thomas*, which asserts: "The disciples said to Jesus, 'We know that you are going to leave us. Who will be our leader?' Jesus said to them, 'No matter where you are, you are to go to James the Just, for whose sake heaven and earth came into being.'"[1] James was revered because Jesus supposedly appointed him as a reliable source of mystical truth.

Several Gnostic writings take the form of secret revelations that James received from his brother after the resurrection. For example, the *Secret Book of James* purports to be a revelation given by Jesus to James and Peter, which James then wrote down in Hebrew. But the heavenly mysteries are not to be spread far and wide. James warns his readers to "endeavor earnestly and take care not to recount this book to many—this which the Savior did not desire to recount to all of us, his twelve disciples. But blessed are those who will be saved through faith in this discourse."[2] Here we find the emphasis on hidden wisdom and salvation through knowledge that so often characterized the Gnostics.

Similarly, the two texts called the *First* and *Second Apocalypse of James* use James as a mouthpiece to convey cryptic sayings from the Lord. And even the text we mentioned in chapter 5, the *Proto-Gospel of James*, conveys themes that fit this overall picture. Although that book isn't full of Gnostic speculations, it does advocate sexual renunciation by going to great lengths to prove Mary's virginity and separation from the world. The ancient evidence shows that some people identified James as a teacher of esoteric wisdom who was devoted to strict bodily self-discipline.

But is that true? Well, yes and no. Even a casual reader of the epistle of James in the New Testament can see that it fits the genre of "wisdom literature." That is, it describes the righteous path of life, the path that only the few who are wise will take. The blessing of God will rest on people like this. So in that sense, we can think of James as a "sage," a teacher of wisdom for those who choose to pursue it. However, the type of wisdom James offers is situated squarely within traditional Jewish ethics. What we don't find in the epistle of James is the sort of mysterious otherworldly sayings that characterized the Gnostics. James's wisdom helps the followers of the one true God live well in the present world.

Furthermore, while James certainly observed a strict moral life, his morality was grounded in the Old Testament, not philosophical renunciation of the evil material world. James's nickname was "the Just" for good reason. Those who knew him in Jerusalem noticed his upright life that fit the pattern of a righteous Jew. For example, the Latin father Jerome recorded some excerpts from the second-century historian Hegesippus, who had done some research on the life of James. Hegesippus says:

> After the apostles, James the brother of the Lord surnamed the Just was made head of the Church at Jerusalem. Many indeed are called James. This one was holy from his mother's womb. He drank neither wine nor strong drink, ate no flesh, never shaved or anointed himself with ointment or bathed. He alone had the privilege of entering the Holy of Holies, since indeed he did not use woolen vestments but linen and went alone into the temple and prayed in behalf of the people, insomuch that his knees were reputed to have acquired the hardness of camels' knees. (NPNF2, vol. 3, *Lives of Illustrious Men* 2)

This passage demonstrates that the historical James must have observed a rigorous lifestyle. However, he wasn't doing it out of a Gnostic mistrust of physical matter. And James certainly didn't advocate celibacy. According to 1 Corinthians 9:5, he had a wife, which would have been the norm in his culture. James was a traditional Jewish man praying and fasting for Israel at the Jerusalem temple, not a mystic purging himself from earthly contamination. The texts that associate him with Gnosticism do not fit the rest of the evidence. We have no good reason to think James would have been connected to Gnostic spirituality. Thus, the persona of the Gnostic James fails the historical test.

James the Ebionite?

In addition to the Gnostics, a second group of ancient people who competed for the legacy of James were the Jewish-Christians who had embraced Jesus but wanted to remain close to the law of Moses. Depending on how close they remained, these folks could be considered either orthodox or heretical. Some ancient believers found a way to incorporate Jewish social patterns into the life of the early church, and in so doing they made a vital contribution to church history. These Christians were centered around the city of Antioch, often with connections to Edessa and the Syrian church as described in the previous chapter.

On the other hand, some Jewish-Christian sectarians considered Jesus as nothing more than a great prophet. Though they identified themselves with His message, they understood Him as an ordinary human being whom God had empowered in a special way to teach the true meaning of the law. The church fathers used the term "Ebionite" to designate this form of Jewish-Christianity. In particular, the term refers to the Jewish-Christian sects that flourished east of the Sea of Galilee and the Jordan River during the ancient period. This movement was condemned as heretical because it denied the divinity of Christ and demanded law-keeping for salvation.

The Ebionites considered James their great hero and founder. Since they viewed Paul with a skeptical eye, the Ebionites appreciated James for seeming to oppose the apostle to the Gentiles who ruthlessly cast aside the entire Old Testament.

Although this caricature of Paul is exaggerated, James certainly did have a pro-Jewish spin on his theology. In Acts 15, we find that while he rejected works salvation, he wanted to retain a few Jewish regulations out of respect for the Mosaic law (vv. 13–21).

Yet the texts that were being read in Ebionite circles went far beyond this, making James into a guardian of all things Jewish. For example, James appears prominently in certain fictional narratives called the *Clementine Homilies*. These writings portray him as a defender of the law against Gentile intruders. One of these texts claims to be a letter in which Peter urges James to protect the true faith from Paul's corruptions. "For some from among the Gentiles have rejected my legal preaching," Peter declares to James, "attaching themselves to [the] lawless and trifling preaching of the man who is my enemy" (ANF, vol. 8, *Epistle of Peter to James* 2). Calling Paul the "enemy" is definitely strong language here! In response to this exhortation, James promises to give the books of Peter's preaching only "to one who is good and religious, and who wishes to teach, and who is circumcised, and faithful" (*E.P.J.* 4). Notice how the Ebionites' version of James equates circumcision with true, faithful religion. It was doctrines like these that made the church fathers view the Ebionites as heretics.

What are we to make of this persona for James? Was he really a Jewish-Christian radical who opposed Paul's gospel of grace? In addressing this matter, we cannot deny that a certain tension existed between the viewpoints of James and Paul. As so often happens in theology, the truth emerged out of the interplay between two doctrinal camps. For example, the famous statement in James 2:24 that "a person is justified by works and not by faith alone" is usually understood to counteract a kind of Pauline extremism that claimed good works were unnecessary in the Christian life. As for Paul, he certainly had a low regard for those he called "the circumcision party." The epistle to the Galatians was written against them, and we should not forget that Paul referred to the Judaizers as "men from James" (Gal. 2:12).

Nevertheless, Paul considered James a "pillar" of the Jerusalem church who offered him the "right hand of fellowship" (2:9). The two men eventually found a way to reconcile their views at the Jerusalem council of Acts 15. Thus, while it is fair to say James tried to do his theology through a Jewish lens, to turn him into an adherent of law-keeping for salvation, or to suggest he denied the deity of Christ, goes beyond the first-century evidence.

Though James was a Jewish-Christian, he worshiped Jesus as the "Lord of glory" (James 2:1) and considered Him the coming Judge of the world (5:7–8). He also welcomed Gentiles into the church and did not demand they be circumcised (Acts 15:5, 19). Therefore, James was no Ebionite. Like the Gnostic James, this persona also fails to withstand historical scrutiny.

James the Bishop of Jerusalem

A third group that attempted to claim the legacy of James was the mainstream Christian community whose leaders we have identified as the early church fathers. These believers quickly developed a form of church government called monepiscopacy. The term refers to the practice of churches being led by one bishop per congregation or urban area, assisted by presbyters who share the pastoral load. Of course, ancient bishops wanted to make sure they stood in "apostolic succession," that is, they could trace their ordination through earlier bishops back to an original apostle of Christ. Therefore it became important to identify the first bishops in each major city—and in Jerusalem, the founding bishop was universally understood to have been James.

The church historian Eusebius describes James as "the brother of the Lord, to whom the episcopal seat at Jerusalem had been entrusted by the apostles" (NPNF2, vol. 1, *C.H.* 2.23.1). Eusebius then provides an excerpt from the same writings by Hegesippus that we mentioned above as being quoted by Jerome. This second-century history book made the noteworthy assertions that James: (1) was dedicated to God from birth; (2) abstained from alcohol and meat; (3) did not cut his hair; (4) denied himself bodily luxuries; (5) entered the "holy place" in linen garments; (6) prayed in the temple so often that his knees became calloused like a camel's; and (7) was called a "bulwark of the people" and "just" (*C.H.* 2.23.4–7). Because this excerpt comes from an early and reliable historian, it is a significant piece of evidence about James. Let us try and understand what it means.

We have already seen that James was not an ascetic Gnostic. How, then, should we interpret his austere lifestyle? Most scholars believe James had undertaken a Nazirite vow, which was an ancient Jewish pledge of devotion to God (Num. 6:1–21). A vow like this would have kept James close to the temple as a focal point of his piety. Although James's linen garments and presence in the "holy place" make it sound like he was a high priest, he actually wasn't of the necessary aristocratic background for that to be true. Nevertheless, he is depicted as having a priestly kind of ministry as he interceded on behalf of Israel.

Because James is so closely associated with the temple and is never said to travel, he probably spent the final years of his life in Jerusalem. Eusebius even claims that James sat on an actual bishop's throne that had been preserved by later generations (*C.H.* 7.19.1), but that is unlikely since the concept of a special chair in the church wasn't established until later.[3] In light of the fact that James rejected the idea of prestigious seats of honor (James 2:3), he probably wouldn't have presided over the church from an episcopal throne.

Even so, James does appear to have been the acknowledged spiritual leader of the Christians in the Holy City. This is the persona that comes closest to historical reality.

LEGACY OF THE EARLY JERUSALEM CHURCH

Therefore, we should picture James as a devout Jewish-Christian shepherding the original church in Jerusalem. Most of these believers were ethnic Jews, so they would have wanted to confess Jesus while retaining their adherence to God's law (much like

Messianic Jews do today). Though the Jerusalem temple would have been an important gathering place for them, they would have met in houses as well. Some of the community may even have continued to meet at Mark's mother's house as described in chapter 2. Things continued along like this for several decades, with James providing steady leadership and interacting with the apostles whenever possible.

But in AD 66, disaster struck. Jewish revolutionaries rebelled against Rome, sparking a bloody war that culminated in the destruction of the temple. According to Eusebius, the Christians at Jerusalem fled the upheaval of those days and relocated in the region beyond the Jordan River (*C.H.* 3.5.3). In this remote area they lost contact with the broader church and became more legalistic in their view of salvation. Soon they began to despise Paul's message of grace and to regard Jesus as a human prophet, not God in the flesh. It is these heretical sects that the church fathers called "Ebionites."

Although they eventually faded off the stage of history, we should note that the Jewish shape of their faith did influence the Syriac-speaking churches of ancient Edessa and Persia. So in a certain sense, we could say the legacy of the Jerusalem church survives today in the Assyrian Church of the East that we encountered in chapter 6.

JAMES'S DEATH AND BURIAL

Where was James during all this turmoil? Did he make the flight across the Jordan with the other Jerusalem believers? The historical evidence unanimously suggests the opposite: that James was killed in Jerusalem just before the church fled the city. A non-Christian witness to this event comes from the Jewish historian Flavius Josephus. He records that in the year we call AD 62, the high priest Ananus assembled the council of judges and "brought before them the brother of Jesus, who was called Christ, whose name was James, and some others; and when he had formed an accusation against them as breakers of the law, he delivered them to be stoned" (ccel.org/ccel/josephus/complete, *Antiquities* 20.9.1). Because this is an early description of what happened to James, and the author had no theological axe to grind, scholars consider it likely to be accurate.

Yet later Christian accounts add some details that may be correct as well. The narrative of Hegesippus describes how the Jews respected James for his piety but demanded to hear what he would say about Jesus. James was allowed to stand on a high place in the temple so all could hear his words. However, when he declared Jesus was sitting in glory at the right hand of God, the authorities realized their error in letting James speak and hurled him to the ground. Since the fall did not kill him, everyone began to stone him, until at last he was struck on the head with a heavy club used by launderers to beat cloth (*C.H.* 2.23.8–18).

While it isn't easy to say exactly what happened or to reconcile the two accounts, we can hypothesize that James's preaching in Jerusalem led to some kind of trial and condemnation, and the hostile atmosphere led to mob violence that the authorities did nothing to prevent.

What happened to the body of James? Like all ancient Jews, the earliest believers would have been concerned for his proper burial. The Hegesippus account says James was buried on the spot of his stoning, and that a "monument" was erected near the temple. This statement is all the more intriguing in light of a recent archaeological discovery from Jerusalem. In 2002, a nondescript limestone ossuary (a box for holding the bones of a dead person) surfaced in the possession of Israeli antiquities collector Oded Golan. The ossuary bore an astounding Aramaic inscription: "James, son of Joseph, brother of Jesus." When this artifact came to light, the archaeological world exploded into controversy. Could this be the earliest physical evidence for James—and even Jesus Himself? Many scholars said yes.

But to complicate the story, the box's owner was suspected of being a forger who made money by linking old objects to biblical narratives. Oded Golan eventually was put on trial before an Israeli court, where insufficient evidence was found to convict him. Today the scholarly community remains divided about the James ossuary. Some consider it a clever fake, while other leading authorities—including Hershel Shanks, editor of the respected journal *Biblical Archaeology Review*—believe the box is authentic. Of course, even if it does come from the first century, the names were common enough that it might not be the actual ossuary of the biblical James. And so the mystery continues.

But in the end, James's status as the Lord's brother shouldn't be something we make a big deal about. How do we know? Because Jesus Himself didn't emphasize it. One time when His disciples informed Him that His family members were waiting outside the door, Jesus expressed His true priorities by saying, "Who are my mother and my brothers?" His blunt answer to His own question is a good reminder to us all: "Whoever does the will of God, he is my brother and sister and mother" (Mark 3:31-35). In other words, to give ear to the Word of the Lord is what brings us into the family of Jesus. Better to be that kind of brother than to have your name carved in stone.

REPORT CARD

JAMES

Was the son of Mary and the half brother of Jesus	A
Was the same man as James of Alphaeus and James the Less	D
Wrote works and conveyed wisdom for Gnostic sects	D-
Was completely opposed to the apostle Paul	F
Practiced a strict moral lifestyle	A-
Led a Jewish-Christian congregation in Jerusalem until his death	A
Was killed by stoning and mob violence	B+
Had his bones collected in the "James ossuary"	C+

A= Excellent, B= Good, C= Average, D= Below average, F= Not passing

CHAPTER 8

THE OTHER APOSTLES

G od's church is like a human a body—and that means some parts must stay hidden under clothing! This somewhat startling observation isn't my own; it's the Bible's. "Our unpresentable parts are treated with greater modesty, which our more presentable parts do not require," the apostle Paul observes (1 Cor. 12:23-24). In this way Paul acknowledges that some people do vital things for the body of Christ but never receive earthly kudos for it. Think of the singer who gives her all to lead worship but will never cut a record. The eloquent wordsmith who encourages others verbally but will never publish a book. The pastor who invests in the lives of broken people but will never headline a trendy conference. Even some of the apostles were like this—such as Andrew, who isn't highly celebrated today, but who led his brother Peter to Christ and changed the world as a result. Just because you aren't famous doesn't mean you don't count.

Let's face it: few Christians could name all twelve of Jesus' disciples. Give it a try and see how you do. Chances are, you'll get stuck halfway through the attempt. But if you're starting to feel guilty about this gap in your knowledge, please don't! The reason

we don't know much about the Twelve—except for a certain few—
is that the Bible itself doesn't give us much information.

SEVEN OTHER DISCIPLES

The disciples of Jesus are listed in Matthew 10:2–4; Mark 3:16–19;
Luke 6:14–16; and Acts 1:13. All of the names in these lists match
up except one. A disciple called Thaddeus is mentioned in the
gospels of Matthew and Mark, while the two-volume work of
Luke–Acts refers to a man named "Judas the son of James." Many
scholars consider Judas/Thaddeus to be the same person (a matter
we will discuss further in a moment). Therefore, excluding Judas
Iscariot who committed suicide after betraying the Lord, and
the four disciples with separate chapters in this book (Matthew,
John, Thomas, and Peter), there are seven other original disciples:
Andrew, James the son of Zebedee, Philip, Bartholomew, James
the son of Alphaeus, Judas Thaddeus, and Simon the Zealot. (In
addition to these, the disciple Matthias was chosen to replace
Judas [Acts 1:26], but Scripture tells us nothing about him, and
church tradition has typically confused him with Matthew; so we
won't be attempting to reconstruct his life in this book.)

Despite the fact that the extra seven disciples are rather obscure
figures in the Bible compared to the more noteworthy five, all
twelve of them must be very important in God's plan, because
Revelation 21:14 states that in the New Jerusalem, "the wall of
the city [will have] twelve foundations, and on them [will be] the
twelve names of the twelve apostles of the Lamb." Jesus Himself
said the twelve disciples would rule over the tribes of Israel (Matt.
19:28; Luke 22:30). So it is worth asking: Who are these other seven
disciples? And what did they do after Acts? Let's list them now
and examine what church tradition has to say about each.

Andrew

As every golfer knows, the windswept coast of eastern Scotland is home to the Royal and Ancient Golf Club of St Andrews. Founded in 1754, the club is the traditional birthplace of this most venerable and frustrating of sports. But why is it called St Andrews? What do Scottish aristocrats in plus-fours and argyle socks have to do with a Jewish fisherman from Galilee? In truth, not much, but the story of Andrew is interesting nonetheless.

According to the Bible, Andrew was Simon Peter's brother and a partner in their fishing enterprise based in Capernaum on the Sea of Galilee (Mark 1:16–20). Andrew even had the privilege of introducing his brother to Jesus Christ (John 1:40–42) — quite the historic moment, if you think about it! Yet beyond these references and a few other casual mentions of Andrew in the Gospels, we aren't told anything else about his life.

At this point, church tradition steps in and tries to offer the rest of the story. The *Acts of Andrew*, a Greek work from the second century, provides a detailed account of the apostle's life and death. Though several scattered fragments remain in various languages and versions, most of that writing is lost today. The text was widely read in ancient times, not only by the orthodox but also the heretics. However, because of certain dubious teachings woven into the narrative, it came to be rejected by the Roman church as unreliable. The text is so obviously legendary that we are forced to doubt whether any of it is true. This mythmaking tendency only intensified over time as fantastic stories of Andrew's miracles among a cannibalistic race became part of his legend (ANF, vol. 8, *Acts of Andrew and Matthias*; *Acts of Peter and Andrew*). Unfortunately, these apocryphal narratives do not give us much insight into the apostle's actual life.

Yet one historical tidbit from the *Acts of Andrew* may be accurate: his ministry in Greece. This location is confirmed by several ancient church fathers, such as Gregory of Nazianzus (NPNF2, vol. 7, *Against the Arians, and Concerning Himself* 11) and Jerome

(NPNF2, vol. 6, *Letter 59, to Marcella* 5). Slightly later traditions also connect Andrew with Asia Minor. Possible corroboration of this comes from the third-century writer Origen, who states that Andrew went to Scythia, a land on the opposite coast of the Black Sea from Asia Minor (NPNF2, vol. 1, *C.H.* 3.1.1–2).

Scythia would have been reachable by ship from territories within the Roman Empire. However, let us remember that Greece and Asia Minor were the exact areas where Paul traveled. If one of Christ's original disciples ministered in the same regions as Paul, why wasn't he ever mentioned in the book of Acts or the Pauline epistles? One reasonable explanation would be that Andrew may have gone to Greece or Asia Minor after Paul's lifetime.

Taken together, the ancient stories about Andrew associate him most strongly with Greece, and in particular the city of Patras in Achaea, the traditional site of his martyrdom. According to the passion narrative attached to the *Acts of Andrew*, a local Roman governor named Aegeates commanded Andrew to worship idols. When Andrew refused, the two began to debate about the meaning of the crucified Christ. At last Aegeates grew fed up and ordered Andrew beaten, then tied to a cross to prolong his suffering. But while hanging on the cross, Andrew's words were so noble that the people demanded his release. Aegeates was forced to agree. However, Andrew rejected these rescue attempts and went to be with God. As for Aegeates, he was so tormented by the devil that he fell from a height and died (ANF, vol. 8, *Acts and Martyrdom of the Holy Apostle Andrew*).

In later versions of the martyrdom story, the cross is described as X-shaped. Eventually the St. Andrew's Cross, or saltire, became a common emblem on Britain's Union Jack, the national flag of Scotland, and many others. Medieval legends recount that Andrew's relics were brought to Scotland in the fourth century, causing the saint to exercise special protection over that country. An old stone tower at St Andrews still marks the spot where the bones were originally placed. The relics were lost during the upheaval of the Reformation, and new ones now rest in an Edinburgh cathedral.

Of course, various parts of the apostle's alleged skeleton also remain in Greece and other places where Andrew is revered today. The Russians even claim Andrew as a patron saint due to his travels to Scythia, and the saltire appears in the flag of the Russian Navy. Yet all of this veneration is based upon little hard evidence. The most we can say about Andrew is that he may have traveled to Greece in the late first century with the message of Jesus Christ.

James the Son of Zebedee

Although it isn't always recognized, the figure of James the Great has left a significant mark on our world, especially in areas where Spanish influence has been strong. Many cities bear his name in the Hispanicized form "Santiago," such as in Chile, Cuba, and the Dominican Republic. All of this is because James is reputed to be buried at the cathedral of Santiago de Compostela, the ornate Spanish shrine that served as the destination for travelers along the greatest of the medieval pilgrimage routes.

Even today, El Camino de Santiago (the Way of St. James) continues to draw religious seekers from around the world. A student of mine recently traveled the route after her graduation, using the arduous foot journey as spiritual preparation for the overseas mission work to which she was called. And like all Camino pilgrims, she visited the crypt that claims to house the relics of James. But does it really?

As we noted in chapter 7, the disciple known in church history as James the Great was the son of Zebedee and the brother of John (Matt. 4:21; Mark 3:17; Luke 5:10). Unlike all the other apostles, we know exactly what happened to him after the time of Christ. Acts 12:1–3 records, "About that time Herod the king laid violent hands on some who belonged to the church. He killed James the brother of John with the sword, and when he saw that it pleased the Jews, he proceeded to arrest Peter also." This event, which happened around the year 44, means James the Great was the first apostolic martyr. Jesus had previously predicted this outcome when He declared, "The cup [of suffering] that I drink you will drink, and with the baptism with which I am baptized, you will be baptized" (Mark 10:39).

But ancient church tradition doesn't tell us much about this James. The earliest testimony comes from the second-century writer Clement of Alexandria, who recounts a story he had heard about James's bold witness on the way to his death. The man assigned to guard him was so moved by the apostle's amazing courage that he declared himself a Christian and joined James in martyrdom (NPNF2, vol. 1, *C.H.* 2.9.1–3). However, the spiritual conversion of the watching pagan captors is a stock element that is often added to martyr stories, so this is more likely a pious embellishment to the Acts 12 narrative than an actual historical event.

Later apocryphal works invent other missionary endeavors for James, but those works aren't given much credence by historians. The most influential stories were the ones that associated James with Spain, where he became a beloved patron saint. A ninth-century text called the *Martyrology of Usuard* attests that a popular shrine for the apostle's relics existed at that time. Another medieval legend relates how the pilgrimage destination at Santiago de Compostela got its start when a monk named Pelagius was guided to James's tomb by a star and heavenly music.

However, the sources behind these legends are too late to be of much value. While there was great devotion to James's supposed relics in medieval Spain, and one source (the seventh-century Latin version of the *Breviarium Apostolorum*) even claims he ministered there prior to his execution in Jerusalem, no reliable evidence connects James the Great with that country. The truth is, we know nothing about his later life except what is recorded in Acts 12:2.

Philip

According to the fourth gospel, Philip was one of Jesus' most earnest followers. He invited Nathanael (= Bartholomew? see below) to meet the Savior for the first time (John 1:45-51), and he also asked Jesus to show him more of the heavenly Father—to which Jesus replied, "Have I been with you so long, and you still do not know me, Philip? Whoever has seen me has seen the Father" (14:8-9).

This disciple had his faith tested at the feeding of the five thousand (6:5-6), and he served as a go-between for some Gentiles who wanted to meet Jesus (12:21-22). Other than these events, and the appearance of his name in the lists of the disciples, we know nothing else about Philip from the Bible.

But perhaps you are remembering that the eighth chapter of Acts describes a Philip who was a great evangelist in Samaria. This man turned his audience away from Simon the Magician toward the true gospel, and he converted the Ethiopian eunuch by reading from the book of Isaiah with him. Wasn't this the apostle Philip? Actually, a close reading of Scripture reveals him to be someone else.

In Acts 6:1-6 we discover that the original disciples appointed seven trustworthy men to supervise food distribution to poor widows; and a new "Philip" is named as one of these seven. Later we learn this Philip had four virgin daughters who prophesied at Caesarea (21:8-9). Therefore, we must distinguish between Philip the Apostle who followed Christ, and Philip the Evangelist who proclaimed the gospel afterward—though church tradition has not always made this important distinction.

The ancient historian Eusebius was one of many who confused the two biblical figures. In his *Church History* he quotes Polycrates, bishop of Ephesus in the late second century, as saying that Philip was "one of the twelve apostles, who fell asleep in Hierapolis" (NPNF2, vol. 8, *C.H.* 5.24.2). Yet this Philip was also said to be the father of "two aged virgin daughters, and another daughter, who lived in the Holy Spirit and now rests at Ephesus" (apparently the fate of the fourth daughter was unknown). Here we can see that Polycrates clearly equated the two Philips, and Eusebius did not dispute it. Other ancient traditions followed this error as well.

The reference to Hierapolis in this passage is also worth noticing. At another place in the *Church History*, Eusebius quotes a source from around AD 200 that similarly claimed Philip's final resting place was the Phrygian city of Hierapolis (*C.H.* 3.31.4–6). A few pages later, Eusebius states that Papias, bishop of Hierapolis, knew where to find Philip's tomb in his city (*C.H.* 3:39.8–9).

An anonymous writing called the *Acts of Philip* likewise presents various apostolic escapades that culminate at Hierapolis (ANF, vol. 8). This text vividly describes Philip's martyrdom around the year 98—although his entrance into paradise is delayed by the Lord because the dying martyr, instead of forgiving his enemies, calls down judgment on them for crucifying him upside down with hooks through his ankles! Despite such fanciful details, the combined witness of texts like these give the Hierapolis tradition for Philip's martyrdom extremely strong attestation. In contrast, certain Gnostic texts that locate Philip in other parts of the empire cannot be accorded the same degree of historical reliability.

Interestingly, a recent archaeological discovery has corroborated the non-Gnostic textual evidence. In the ruins of ancient Hierapolis (near modern Pamukkale, Turkey), the remains of a fifth-century martyr shrine are still visible. This building was once a domed structure adorned with beautiful marble and mosaics. Though it was constructed in honor of Philip, it does not appear to have ever housed his relics. But in a stunning archaeological discovery from 2011, the first-century tomb of Philip himself was discovered in the ruins of an adjacent church about forty yards away. These two churches are pictured on an ancient bronze stamp that was used to mark bread for liturgical usage. The scene on the bread stamp depicts Philip standing in Hierapolis between the domed martyrium and another church with a cross on top—evidently the one that housed his tomb. Philip's bones, however, were not discovered in his grave. Medieval tradition says the relics were moved to Rome long ago and now reside in the church of the Twelve Holy Apostles just a few blocks from Rome's famous Trevi Fountain.

Though the validity of those bones is doubtful, we have nonetheless found good ancient evidence for the presence of a biblical "Philip" in Hierapolis. So now we must ask, which Philip was it—the Apostle or Evangelist? It could have been either, since they were so quickly confused. However, now that the first-century tomb of Philip has been securely located in Hierapolis, the early testimony of the local bishop must prove decisive. Bishop Papias—who made a close study of everything pertaining to the apostles—declares that he not only knew of the tomb, he actually knew the prophetic daughters of Philip (NPNF2, vol. 8, *C.H.* 3.39.9). These daughters had told him about a certain woman who had been raised from the dead (identified elsewhere as the wife of Manaen from Acts 13:1). Since Papias was personally acquainted with the Spirit-filled daughters, it must have been Philip the Evangelist mentioned in the book of Acts, not the apostle from the Gospels, whose martyr's tomb was revered at Hierapolis.

This means, in turn, we can say very little about what happened to the disciple of Jesus named Philip. The church father Clement of Alexandria recorded the testimony of an earlier authority who claimed Philip the Apostle did not die a martyr's death (ANF, vol. 2, *Stromata* 4.9). In all likelihood, that is correct. Indeed, it is possible Philip never even left the Holy Land. But whatever may have happened to this original follower of Jesus, we may be certain of one thing: his earnest request to behold the Father's glory has now been perfectly fulfilled.

Bartholomew

The rear wall of the Sistine Chapel in Rome is decorated with one of the world's greatest works of art: Michelangelo's *Last Judgment*. Among the many arresting sights in that fresco is a bald, muscular man holding a knife in one hand and his removed skin in the other. Most historians have suggested Michelangelo inserted his own weary features into the drooping skin to symbolize the toll the massive artwork had taken on him. Whether or not that is true, there is no question the saint depicted here is Bartholomew, who is said to have been martyred by being flayed alive. But did such a gruesome and painful death really befall this apostle?

The disciple called Bartholomew is always mentioned alongside Philip in the Synoptic Gospels (e.g., Matt. 10:3). In contrast, the gospel of John never makes reference to Bartholomew. Yet this gospel does mention a certain "Nathanael of Cana" who is a close friend of Philip (John 1:45–49; 21:2). For this reason, many scholars consider Bartholomew and Nathanael to be the same person. About him, the Lord Jesus exclaimed, "Behold, an Israelite indeed, in whom there is no deceit!" (John 1:47).

Though the apocryphal texts about Bartholomew locate his ministry in various places, the strongest line of tradition connects him—like Doubting Thomas and Judas Thaddeus—with missionary work in India (e.g., ANF, vol. 5, *Hippolytus on the Twelve Apostles* 6). But as we saw in chapter 6, the ancient Romans were vague in their description of eastern geography. The term "India" could cover a lot of territory. It sometimes referred to the Parthian (or Persian) Empire, which included regions that are today in Pakistan, Afghanistan, and Iran. In other words, Bartholomew tends to be associated with the Syrian and Persian peoples east of the Roman Empire. These lands are not far from Armenia, where other legends soon developed around the person of Bartholomew. However, as with Thomas, we cannot be certain that Bartholomew's evangelistic work reached as far as the modern nation of India.

Among the ancient sources that locate Bartholomew's ministry in the Parthian or "Indian" context, one of the most important is the *Martyrdom of the Holy and Glorious Apostle Bartholomew* (ANF, vol. 8). The text opens with the declaration that India is divided into three parts; and it is to the farthest section, a land surrounded by oceans and darkness, that "the holy Bartholomew the apostle of Christ went, and took up his quarters." Yet this document, like others from the ancient period, makes no mention of the apostle's death by flaying. Instead, "the [evil] king rent the purple in which he was clothed, and ordered the holy apostle Bartholomew to be beaten with rods; and after having been thus scourged, to be beheaded." Only within church traditions from Armenia after AD 600 does the flaying enter the story.

Today in a remote part of eastern Turkey, the ruins of a medieval Armenian monastery still stand on the supposed site of Bartholomew's horrific martyrdom (though other places claim to be the actual site as well). The flaying legend quickly made its way into other Christian texts, showing up in western Europe in the seventh-century *Breviarium Apostolorum* and the writings of the Spanish theologian Isidore of Seville.

The sensational medieval bestseller called the *Golden Legend* helped spread Bartholomew's story even further. Now firmly ensconced in the Western imagination, the flaying of St. Bartholomew became a common scene in late medieval and Renaissance art. However, the event has no attestation during the first six centuries of the Christian church.

So then, all that can be said with any degree of plausibility is that Bartholomew may have moved eastward along the same trajectory as Thomas and Judas Thaddeus. The Indian connection is supported by the testimony of the second-century Egyptian scholar Pantaenus, whose travels among Indian Christians revealed that "Bartholomew, one of the apostles, had preached to them, and left with them the writing of Matthew in the Hebrew language, which they had preserved till that time" (NPNF2, vol. 1, *C.H.* 5.10.3; see also NPNF2, vol. 3, Jerome, *Lives of Illustrious Men* 36). This early piece of evidence suggests that Bartholomew had perhaps visited India; or more likely, a Jewish-Christian gospel connected with Bartholomew was known along the southern coast of India where Pantaenus made his visit.

Yet Indian Christianity was normally in close contact with the church of Syria and Persia. Taken together, the various sources demonstrate that Bartholomew was remembered as a pioneering figure in the eastern, Syriac-speaking church (today called the Assyrian Church of the East). From there his legend spread to nearby Armenia, where he was again adopted as a patron saint and founder.

However, his death as a martyr by flaying is not well attested; and even the story of his martyrdom by more conventional methods has the ring of legend to it. Though it is probable that Bartholomew evangelized the Persian east, and he might even have reached India, nothing else can be said about him with historical confidence.

James the Son of Alphaeus

Evidence about the postbiblical life of the disciple known as James the son of Alphaeus depends on his identification with another biblical James. As we have seen, ancient church tradition equated the disciple who was the son of Alphaeus with James the Less of Mark 15:40 and James the brother of Jesus who wrote the New Testament epistle that bears his name. For example, a work attributed to the third-century church father Hippolytus (though actually from a later time) states, "James the son of Alphaeus, when preaching in Jerusalem, was stoned to death by the Jews, and was buried there beside the temple" (ANF, vol. 5, *Hippolytus on the Twelve Apostles* 9).

Clearly this author, whoever he was, considered James the son of Alphaeus to be the same man as James the Just. However, this view is probably not correct—which means, in turn, that we don't know anything about the son of Alphaeus. The early Christian stories that spoke of "James" intended to describe other New Testament personalities with the identical name.

Among the New Testament Jameses, the only one about whom we know much at all is the brother of the Lord. In contrast, the son of Zebedee is virtually lost to us as a historical figure. He certainly did not go to Spain. The only thing we know about him is his martyrdom under Herod Agrippa (Acts 12:2). And just as we have no biography for the son of Zebedee, so we are left with no real knowledge about the son of Alphaeus either. These two disciples named James simply disappeared from recorded history after their biblical narratives ended.

Judas Thaddeus

The precise identity of this biblical figure is a matter of debate. As we noted earlier, Matthew and Mark both mention a disciple named Thaddeus. However, Luke refers to him as *Ioudas* in Greek, which can be translated either as Judas or Jude in English. To explain this discrepancy of identification, most commentators think the disciple probably went by two names. He was called Judas Thaddeus, which means something like Judas the Stout-Hearted. Since the name Judas had become tainted by association with the traitorous disciple, the gospel writers Matthew and Mark decided to use the nickname Thaddeus alone to identify this man (Matt. 10:3; Mark 3:18).

But Luke—always a more precise and technical historian—recorded the official name of *Ioudas* in his writings. Similarly, John 14:22 distinguishes this Judas from the traitor by calling him "Judas, *not Iscariot.*" Yet when we put all the evidence together, it appears that Judas Thaddeus was a single individual—one of the twelve disciples of the Lord.

There is, of course, a New Testament epistle authored by someone named Jude. Is this the same person as the disciple Judas Thaddeus? Catholic traditions about "St. Jude," the popular patron saint of hopeless causes, actually do equate the letter-writer with the disciple of Christ.

Although this is not absolutely impossible, it is something of a stretch. The problem is that the author of the epistle calls himself "Jude . . . the *brother* of James" (v. 1). But when Judas Thaddeus is called "Judas of James" in Luke 6:16 and Acts 1:13, the designation would normally indicate a father/son relationship, not a brotherly one. Therefore, the preferable view is that the epistle of Jude was written by a different man, a sibling of Jesus and James named *Ioudas* (and Matt. 13:55/Mark 6:3 prove the Lord did have a brother by that name).

This means the disciple Judas Thaddeus was someone else: a member of the Twelve, though neither a brother of Jesus nor a biblical author.

So if Judas Thaddeus didn't pen a New Testament document, what did he do for his Savior after Acts? The ancient church traditions about this figure tend to point eastward into the Syrian and Persian lands that we have already associated with Thomas and Bartholomew. For example, in the apocryphal *Passion of Simon and Jude*, Judas Thaddeus travels with Simon the Zealot to Babylon, where they debate with the Persian magi. The characters proceed through a series of adventures until at last they are martyred by the priests of the sun god. But because this fourth-century text appears to be duplicating or retelling earlier fiction about other apostles, modern scholars don't give it much historical credence.

Another story that may associate Judas Thaddeus with the Syrian and Persian church is recounted by Eusebius (NPNF2, vol. 1, *C.H.* 1.13). According to this tale, the diseased ruler of the Syrian city of Edessa, King Abgar V, sent Jesus an urgent request to come and heal him. Although Jesus politely declined due to His other ministry obligations, He promised to send one of His disciples very soon (and in a later version of the legend, the Lord even allows the king's messenger to paint a picture of His face). After the ascension, the disciple Thomas commissioned someone named Thaddeus to heal Abgar. Eusebius is clear that this person is not one of the inner Twelve, but one of the seventy-two disciples who followed Jesus (Luke 10:1–24). Nevertheless, church tradition has sometimes confused this Thaddeus of Edessa (or Mar Addai, as he is called in Syriac) with the disciple Judas Thaddeus. Probably there was an ancient Christian leader named Thaddeus who was associated with Edessa, and since Judas Thaddeus bore the same name, the two figures got combined.

In light of the fact that such legends proliferated in the Syriac-speaking church, the most we can say about the disciple Judas

Thaddeus is that he, like Thomas and Bartholomew, may have moved eastward toward Edessa and ministered in the regions of Syria and Persia. However, since certain men with similar names were mistakenly equated with him—either the letter-writer Jude or Thaddeus of Edessa—it is equally possible that the biblical apostle Judas Thaddeus never even left his homeland. In the end, we cannot know much for sure about him.

Simon the Zealot

If you thought piecing together the five Jameses of the New Testament was complicated, you may be dismayed to hear there were *nine* different Simons in the Bible. However, take heart; we aren't going to try and sort them out here.

The one man on whom we will focus is called Simon the Zealot in Luke–Acts, and Simon the Cananaean in Matthew and Mark. Though this may seem like yet another case of misidentification, the solution is quite simple. The term "Cananaean" is nothing but an Aramaic loan-word that means "Zealot." In ancient Israel, the Zealots were a revolutionary political party that played a prominent role in the outbreak of the Jewish uprising against Rome in AD 66. Such an affiliation may seem surprising for a follower of the Prince of Peace who commanded us to turn the other cheek. However, in the time of Jesus' ministry, a "zealot" wasn't necessarily someone plotting armed rebellion as happened in the 60s. While excessive zeal certainly did exist early in the first century, and that could often have political ramifications, sometimes the word simply indicated a Jewish group with intense devotion to the Lord and His law (e.g., Acts 21:20; Gal. 1:14). The truth is, Simon's zealous nature can be considered to have fit quite well with Jesus' own spiritual outlook (John 2:17).

The church traditions about Simon are spread all over the place—literally. He shows up in Jerusalem, Samaria, Egypt, North Africa, Edessa, Persia, Babylon, the eastern Black Sea region, and even Britain. Furthermore, these traditions are primarily from the fourth century and beyond, which is the exact time when veneration of the apostles' tombs was exploding in the church. It seems no one really knew where Simon went, so he was one of the few original disciples still up for grabs in the early Middle Ages. Whatever city could establish a connection to him would gain the prestige of an apostolic lineage.

We have already seen that the fourth-century *Passion of Simon and Jude* places him in Babylon, but this account is certainly fictitious. In contrast to sending him to such a distant locale, Simon is equated with a certain Symeon who succeeded James as the next bishop of Jerusalem (NPNF2, vol. 1, *C.H.* 3.11.1–2; see also ANF, vol. 5, *Hippolytus on the Twelve Apostles* 11). This man was understood as the brother/cousin of Jesus named Simon mentioned in Matthew 13:55 and Mark 6:3. It is supposed that when James died, the family of Jesus appointed this Simon to take his place. However, the equating of Simon the Zealot with Symeon/Simon of Jerusalem is doubtful because the Zealot was one of the Twelve, whereas the brothers of Jesus were not His followers (John 7:5). The Bible never gives us any reason to conclude these two figures were the same person.

Thus, Simon the Zealot joins Philip and the two Jameses as disciples whose activities after Acts are a complete mystery to us. The information about Andrew, Bartholomew, and Judas Thaddeus isn't much better. All we can do is make educated guesses about the regions where they ministered. Although Acts 1:8 affirms that Jesus' disciples (excluding Judas Iscariot, of course) would evangelize "to the end of the earth," history doesn't actually tell us what happened to seven out of the eleven faithful apostles. Even so, while these particular members of Christ's body may be hidden to our eyes, we will no doubt learn of great deeds and heroic acts of Christian devotion when all is finally revealed.

Yet some of the original disciples did go on to leave a more concrete mark on the historical record: Matthew, John, Thomas, and

Peter. We have already examined the ancient traditions pertaining to the first three of these. As you are probably aware, the stories about the fourth are even more substantial. It is to Simon Peter—the rock of the church and Prince of the Apostles—that we must now turn.

REPORT CARD

THE OTHER DISCIPLES		
	Andrew evangelized Greece	B-
	James the Great went to Spain	F
	James the Great is buried at Santiago de Compostela	D-
	Philip (the Apostle) went to Hierapolis	D
	Bartholomew ministered in the eastern, Syriac-speaking world	B+
	James the son of Alphaeus was the same person as James the Lord's brother	D
	Judas Thaddeus ministered in the eastern, Syriac-speaking world	C+
	Simon the Zealot was the second bishop of Jerusalem	D

A= Excellent, B= Good, C= Average, D= Below average, F= Not passing

CHAPTER 9

PETER

If you were to consider the most influential words ever uttered, what statements would make it onto your top ten list? Perhaps some of them would be political, such as this one from the Declaration of Independence: "We hold these truths to be self-evident, that all men are created equal, that they are endowed by their Creator with certain unalienable Rights, that among these are Life, Liberty, and the Pursuit of Happiness." Certainly those words have meant freedom for numerous people. Yet even if a few political or inspirational quotes were to make it on your list, the majority would need to be religious; for it is religion that has had the most enduring impact on humankind over the millennia, for good as well as for ill. Among the religious quotes, we would have to include—in fact, this would be my number-one pick—Matthew 28:6, "He is not here, for he has risen." It was the resurrection of Jesus Christ that launched the global Christian faith and all that it represents.

✠

However, a close runner-up on my list would be another verse from Matthew: "And I tell you, you are Peter, and on this rock

I will build my church, and the gates of hell shall not prevail against it. I will give you the keys of the kingdom of heaven, and whatever you bind on earth shall be bound in heaven, and whatever you loose on earth shall be loosed in heaven" (16:18-19). I think you can probably guess why this statement is so important. These words of Jesus led to the belief that the pope is the leader of the Roman Catholic Church—a two-thousand-year-old institution whose influence on world history has been incalculable. The Galilean fisherman named Peter has indirectly affected billions of people across the ages by being designated the "first bishop of Rome."

PETER'S PROMINENCE IN THE EARLY CHURCH

Even those Christians who do not believe in the Roman papacy must still marvel at Peter's prominent role in the Bible. He is mentioned seventy-five times in the Synoptic Gospels, thirty-five times in John, and 181 times in the New Testament as a whole. Peter was one of Jesus' most intimate companions, along with the two brothers James the Great and the apostle John.

But it was Peter whom Jesus commissioned to lead the fledgling church. In Luke 22:31-34, Jesus declared at the Last Supper that Satan wanted to sift Peter like wheat and cause him to deny his Lord. Even so, Peter was tasked—after repenting from his great failure—with the job of strengthening the Christian believers.

Likewise in John 21:15-17, Peter was asked three times whether he truly loved Jesus. Upon replying "Yes, Lord, you know that I love you," he was ordered in three different ways to shepherd the flock of God.

One does not have to be a Roman Catholic to discern the foundational importance of Peter in the early church. All we have to do is listen to the words of Christ Himself. It is because of statements like these that the apostle Paul could claim God's household is "built on the foundation of the apostles and prophets, Christ Jesus himself being the cornerstone" (Eph. 2:20).

And yet, despite Peter's prominent role in the Bible, we don't have as detailed a biography for him as we might like. He makes it farther into the book of Acts than the other disciples, most of whom disappear in the second chapter as soon as the Holy Spirit descends. Unlike them, Peter remains an important character for much of the subsequent narrative. But even he vanishes halfway through the book. In Acts 15, after making a speech at the Jerusalem council, Peter is never mentioned again. This happened around AD 49. Any claims about the later activities of Peter must therefore be deduced from vague hints within other biblical books, or be drawn from extrabiblical traditions about the apostle.

So let us turn our attention to these sources now. We will first examine the epistles of 1 and 2 Peter for evidence about the author's life, then see what we can learn from the writings—and the rocks!—of the ancient church.

MINISTERING HERE AND THERE

We have already learned in chapter 2 that Peter was acquainted with a wealthy woman named Mary, the mother of Mark, whose family home was the apostles' base of operations in Jerusalem (Acts 12:12). It was straight to this house that Peter went after he miraculously escaped from prison in AD 44. We do not know exactly what Peter did next. He simply "departed and went to another place" (12:17)—not a bad idea for a recent jailbreaker who just saw his fellow apostle James be put to death.

But sometime between the prison release and Paul's writing of the letter to the Galatians in 48 or 49, Peter visited Antioch, where he had a dispute with Paul about the place of the Jewish law in the church (Gal. 2:11–14; Acts 15:1–2). This tells us that Peter was active in ministry outside of Palestine, though he returned to the Holy City in time for the important council of Acts 15. And according to Acts 9:31–32, Peter was also ministering "here and there" among all the new churches of Judea, Galilee, and Samaria at various times. So as far as we can tell from the New Testament, Peter spent the decades of the 30s and 40s in the eastern Mediterranean world, primarily at Jerusalem.

It is only with the appearance of Peter's two epistles that we get any hint of his ministry farther afield. Conservative scholars date these letters in the early 60s, which means we know nothing from Scripture about what Peter may have been doing during the 50s.[1] However, one potential problem with using the epistles as evidence for Peter's whereabouts is that nearly all liberal scholars agree these two works were written by other individuals who pretended to be Peter at a later time.

This may sound strange, but the theory isn't as far-fetched as it may first appear. Numerous texts by Petrine imitators actually were written in the ancient period, so theoretically, these two letters could be examples of such writings. On the other hand, both of these letters explicitly identify the author as the apostle Peter in their opening verses. For an author to falsify his identity and represent himself as Peter would seem to violate the truthfulness of Scripture.

But even if we set aside concerns about biblical inerrancy, good scholarly method requires that theories about deception lurking behind historical texts must be based on overwhelming evidence to contradict the plain assertion of authorship. Many conservative scholars have found such evidence lacking for 1 and 2 Peter. Although there are plausible arguments on both sides of the debate, the present book will align with those who make the case for Petrine authorship of both epistles.[2]

Peter's First Epistle

The first epistle of Peter was addressed to the churches of several adjacent provinces that formed a large block within Asia Minor (1:1). Some scholars believe Peter may have visited these lands among his travels, which would explain why he is writing to the believers there. This is certainly possible, though it cannot be proven. A more concrete biographical clue comes in 5:13, when

Peter declares in closing, "She who is at Babylon, who is likewise chosen, sends you greetings." What does Peter mean by "she who is at Babylon"? Different theories have been suggested, including the notion that Peter had traveled to the actual city of Babylon on the Euphrates River.

However, there is no real evidence for this, and it is quite a stretch. Modern commentators instead are nearly unanimous in claiming that the expression is a cryptic reference to the Christian community at Rome. Since Babylon was the place of exile in the Old Testament (e.g., in the books of 2 Kings or Jeremiah), Peter was probably saying that the Roman Christians sent warm greetings because they could identify with the letter's recipients as fellow exiles from their true heavenly homeland. Babylon was also a notoriously wicked city, which is why it could symbolize Rome (as it does in Revelation 14:8). So what this verse tells us about Peter is that he probably wrote from Rome, although the exact time period is hard to determine.

Peter's Second Epistle

Among all the New Testament books, 2 Peter is the hardest to attribute to its stated author. Even more than 1 Peter, the second epistle resembles the forged Petrine works of a later period. In addition, the very earliest church fathers seem to be unaware of this epistle; and when it does surface at last, it is viewed with skepticism before finally being accepted as genuine. Yet upon closer examination, the idea that Peter actually authored this epistle is not as preposterous as some scholars declare. Its very different Greek style from 1 Peter can be explained by the theory of scribal assistance that we mentioned when discussing Mark's role as an interpreter.[3]

Assuming that Peter did indeed provide the essential content of this letter to a scribe, it is interesting to discover his assertion in 1:14 that "the putting off of my body will be soon, as our Lord Jesus Christ made clear to me." This is probably a reference to Jesus' declaration to Peter in John 21:18 that "when you were young, you used to dress yourself and walk wherever you wanted, but when you are old, you will stretch out your hands, and another will dress you and carry you where you do not want to go." As we will see in a moment, this language describes violent death under compulsion. Taken together, these two verses show that Peter was aware of his imminent execution when he composed his second epistle. Therefore, the two Petrine letters suggest—though they do not explicitly claim—that their author was martyred at Rome.

PETER'S MARTYRDOM

As we consider the possibility of Peter's Roman martyrdom, we must first take a closer look at John's gospel before proceeding to the extrabiblical evidence. In John 13:36-38, Peter asks, "Lord, where are you going?" to which Jesus answers, "Where I am going you cannot follow me now, but you will follow afterward." Confused, Peter then blurts out, "Lord, why can I not follow you now? I will lay down my life for you." But Jesus' reply is emphatic: "Will you lay down your life for me? Truly, truly, I say to you, the rooster will not crow till you have denied me three times." Notice that in this exchange, the Lord says Peter will "follow afterward" (not now) in His footsteps—and in context, we can see that Peter's costly discipleship will require "laying down his life." In other words, this is a prediction of a martyr's death.

The second important passage is John 21:18-19, which, as we just noted, is the prophecy that Peter seems to have had in mind when he said he would be "putting off" his earthly body very soon. This Johannine text (see above for its quotation) is intriguing because it uses the actual language of crucifixion. The expression "stretch out your hands" was a common way of speaking about the extension of a victim's arms on a Roman cross. Furthermore, the elderly Peter is being led under judicial constraint, no longer free to go where he wishes as in his youth.[4] That the apostle John and the scribal community that assisted him understood Jesus' statement in 21:18 as a prediction of crucifixion is quite clear from the explanatory comment provided in verse 19: "This [Jesus] said to show by what kind of death [Peter] was to glorify God." By the time John's gospel was written, the early church knew that Jesus' prediction about Peter had indeed come true; the parenthetical remark highlights Jesus' ability to foretell the future.

Upside Down on a Roman Cross?

Since the early Christians were aware that Peter had followed in the footsteps of the Savior to the same kind of death, it wasn't long before fictional narratives emerged that purported to recount the whole epic story. These tales are filled with holy saints and vanquished heretics, giving us reasons to view them critically. Yet just because the texts have a legendary, even lurid, flavor doesn't mean they don't have a historical kernel of truth. The trick is to separate fact from fiction!

In the early second century, a collection of oral folklore began to solidify into a narrative trajectory now called the *Acts of Peter*.[5] In addition to such thrilling episodes as a duel between Peter and the heretic Simon Magus, in which Peter causes the flying Simon to crash and burn (chapters 31–32), we also find a detailed account of Peter's martyrdom (chapters 33–41). Emperor Nero is the villain in the background of the story, which proves the second-century Christians believed Peter died during that ruler's reign.

As the story unfolds, we see Nero's henchmen calling for Peter's execution because he convinced their wives and lovers to adopt sexual abstinence. At this point we discover the first outright statement that Peter was crucified on a cross—and also that it was in an upside-down posture. However, the *Acts of Peter* makes no mention of the pious concern that is so often quoted as the reason for Peter being turned head-downward: his sense of unworthiness to be crucified like his Master. That explanation shows up in a much later edition of the story attributed to a certain "Hegesippus" around 370,[6] but the original reason for requesting an upside-down crucifixion was quite different.[7] As Peter waxes eloquent while hanging on the cross, his position visually illustrates his Gnostic-themed speech about the spiritual inversion of the human race.

Neither of these explanations is credible at all. Peter may well have been crucified upside down, for the Romans were known to do this. Since the martyrdom story in the *Acts of Peter* was already developing in the early second century, it might have been recording an actual eyewitness remembrance. However, the victims of Roman crucifixion were not given the chance to make requests about the method of their impalement. The intent was to shame them in a grotesque way, not accomodate their wishes. Therefore, the upside-down crucifixion of Peter is historically plausible, though not for any spiritual reasons.

Nero and the Christians

The mention of Nero in the *Acts of Peter* is one of the places where the legends of Peter's martyrdom intersect with recorded history. After a terrible fire ravaged Rome in AD 64, the decadent Emperor Nero was suspected of intentionally setting the blaze so he could clear urban space for his sumptuous new palace and remake the city for his own glory. Concerned about the nasty rumors, Nero sought a scapegoat to blame, and Christians—widely disdained by the populace—seemed like easy targets. The emperor's fierce persecution of the Roman church is attested in a famous passage from the pagan historian Tacitus:

> First, then, the confessed members of the sect were arrested; next, on their disclosures, vast numbers were convicted, not so much on the count of arson as for hatred of the human race. And derision accompanied their end: they were covered with wild beasts' skins and torn to death by dogs; or they were fastened on crosses, and, when daylight failed, were burned to serve as lamps by night. Nero had offered his Gardens for the spectacle, and gave an exhibition in his Circus, mixing with the crowd in the habit of a charioteer,

or mounted on his [racing chariot]. Hence, in spite of a guilt which had earned the most exemplary punishment, there arose a sentiment of pity, due to the impression that they were being sacrificed not for the welfare of the state but to the ferocity of a single man.[8]

This passage does not, of course, mention Peter by name. However, we do learn that one location where Nero tormented the Christians for his sadistic pleasure was the circus in his imperial gardens. This is a reference to the Circus of Gaius and Nero, which lay outside the city proper, and so was the only Roman racetrack to escape destruction by fire. We will return to this structure and its relevance to Peter shortly.

In the years following the Great Fire of Rome, many Christian texts and authors attest to the death of Peter in the capital city during the reign of Nero. We have already seen that the second-century *Acts of Peter* does so. Other contemporaneous evidences include:

- *First Epistle of Clement* 5, "Through envy and jealousy, the greatest and most righteous pillars [of the Church] have been persecuted and put to death. Let us set before our eyes the illustrious apostles. Peter . . . when he had at length suffered martyrdom, departed to the place of glory due to him" (ANF, vol. 1). Here we see Clement, a first-century bishop in Rome, stating his belief that Peter suffered death locally. Although the Greek participle translated as "suffered martyrdom" could simply refer to bearing witness, the context indicates that Clement had persecution and judicial execution in mind.

- *Ascension of Isaiah* 4:2–3, "Beliar the great ruler, the king of this world, will descend, who hath ruled it since it came into being; yea, he will descend from his firmament in the likeness of a man, a lawless king, the slayer of his mother. . . . [This king] will persecute the plant which the Twelve Apostles of the Beloved have planted. Of the

Twelve, one will be delivered into his hands"[9] This text is an apocalyptic writing of the early second century. It pictures Nero, who was suspected of having deviously killed his mother, Agrippina, as a revived antichrist who returns to earth to persecute the church in the form of the demon Beliar (see 2 Cor. 6:15). The only one of the original twelve disciples ever connected to Nero was Peter, so this text appears to be prophetically interpreting that event.

• Dionysius of Corinth, *Letter to the Romans*, "For both [Peter and Paul] planted and likewise taught us in our Corinth. And they taught together in like manner in Italy, and suffered martyrdom at the same time" (NPNF2, vol. 1, *C.H.* 2.25.8). Writing around AD 170 to the Roman church, the bishop of Corinth wants to unite the two congregations around the fact that both had been evangelized by Peter and Paul.[10] Dionysius clearly believed the two most eminent apostles had been martyred in Italy. His appeal to these founding figures as a basis for unity would have carried extra weight with the Roman Christians because at that time, grave memorials for Peter and Paul had just recently been constructed at Rome (see below).

• Irenaeus of Lyons, *Against Heresies* 3.1.1, "Matthew also issued a written Gospel among the Hebrews in their own dialect, while Peter and Paul were preaching at Rome, and laying the foundations of the Church. After their departure, Mark, the disciple and interpreter of Peter, did also hand down to us in writing what had been preached by Peter" (ANF, vol. 1). We have already examined this text in our chapter on Mark. There we noted that it describes Mark's written account of Jesus as a necessary aid to the memory of the ancient church once the oral preaching of Peter and Paul came to an end with their "departure" (i.e., their deaths). Although Irenaeus does not explicitly mention martyrdom, he claims that Peter and Paul worked together in Rome, then shared a common "exit from the stage" at the same moment (which is what the Greek word for departure literally means). This is widely understood as a reference to the two apostles' joint martyrdom in Rome.

- Tertullian, *Prescription Against Heretics* 36, "Since, moreover, you are close upon Italy, you have Rome. . . . How happy is its church, on which the apostles poured forth all their doctrine along with their blood! where Peter endures a passion like his Lord's!" (ANF, vol. 3). Writing at the dawn of the third century, Tertullian states that Peter's passion was similar to Christ's, that is, it was by means of crucifixion. And once more, this event is said to have happened at Rome.

In light of all this historical evidence, we can affirm that a Roman connection for the apostle Peter is well established. He ministered there for an unknown period of time, possibly over the span of two decades or more. There is no intrinsic reason why the reports of his arrival during the reign of Claudius in the 40s could not be accurate, though of course we need not assume he continuously stayed in the capital city and never traveled anywhere else.[11] The apostle Paul records that Peter was an itinerant preacher who traveled about (1 Cor. 9:5). Wherever his pastoral work took place, Peter's years of fruitful ministry culminated with his death by crucifixion at the hands of Nero.

The Great Fire of Rome occurred in July of 64, and we can imagine that it may have taken some time for the chaos to settle until the Christians could be rounded up for punishment. Therefore, we should probably date the death of Peter to the year 65, or maybe a little afterward (though not much later, since Nero died in the chaotic year of 68). As far as the exact location where this crucifixion occurred, the circus mentioned by Tacitus would be the most likely place to execute such a prominent Christian as Peter. And as it turns out, the convoluted tale of Peter's mortal remains is inextricably tied to Nero's circus that once stood on the Vatican Field at Rome. It is to this field that we must now pay a visit.

THE BURIAL OF PETER

The Vatican Field (*Ager Vaticanus*) was originally a swampy lowland across the Tiber River from the walled city of Rome, nestled between two hills, the Vatican and the Janiculum. In the first century AD, the emperor Gaius, more commonly known as Caligula, made his mother's lush gardens at the base of the Vatican Hill the site of a new circus, which was an oblong structure with seats for watching entertainments such as chariot racing. Caligula decorated the central spine around which the horses ran with a stolen Egyptian obelisk. The granite spike was later moved from this location to the center of St. Peter's Square, where it still stands today.

Next to the circus (which Nero subsequently embellished), across an avenue leading into the city, was a graveyard used especially by poor immigrants from the east. As best we can determine, after Nero's sadistic persecution of the Christians abated, some brave believers requested the body of Peter from the judicial officials (just as had been done for Jesus),[12] then buried the revered apostle in the nearby cemetery.

Over the years, however, more expensive tombs began to spring up in the area, until the region became a "necropolis" or city of the dead. We know that some of these rich tombs eventually belonged to Christians, for a mosaic adorning one of them shows Christ rising in a chariot toward heaven like a sun god.

Trophies

As these later tombs began to encroach upon the simple grave that the Christians remembered as belonging to Peter, a small courtyard was established to identify and preserve the important location. The actual burial spot was marked by a niche in a red plastered wall, with two small decorative columns supporting a stone slab as a kind of canopy. A pastor in Rome named Caius, writing around AD 200, declared in a burst of local pride, "And I can show the trophies of the apostles. For if you choose to go to the Vatican or to the Ostian Road, you will find the trophies of those who founded this church" (ANF, vol. 5, *Fragments of Caius*).[13] This testimony tells us that by the late second century, the graves of both Peter and Paul (on the Vatican Field and the Ostian Road respectively) were marked by "trophies," that is, monuments of victory for the slain martyrs.

Archaeological excavations carried out by the Roman Catholic Church have located Peter's victory monument directly beneath the altar of today's St. Peter's Basilica. The niche in the red wall, once adorned with columns and a canopy, has been rediscovered. Ancient stamps on the drain tiles of nearby construction confirm that this trophy was erected around 160. Thus, within a century or so of Peter's burial—which is only one generation removed from young people who could have seen the apostle with their own eyes—the local Christians had marked the grave with a unique monument.[14]

After the establishment of the Vatican trophy, the location was never again forgotten, and is well known even today. This is because when Emperor Constantine rose to power in the early fourth century and began to sponsor church architecture, a majestic basilica was constructed to commemorate the grave of Peter in a more substantial way. The ancient builders cut a large platform into the Vatican Hill and extended it outward with massive retaining walls. All the tombs of the necropolis were covered with rubble except one: the grave marked by the trophy.

On top of the new platform, a church was erected that soon became the focal point of Western Christendom—and of course, the church's altar was situated directly over the trophy. This "Old St. Peter's," as it has come to be called, lasted for nearly 1,200 years until the time of the Italian Renaissance. By then it was in disrepair and about to fall down. The Renaissance popes demolished it and rebuilt a new church over the course of the sixteenth century, topped by the beautiful dome of the artist and architect Michelangelo.

A giant Latin inscription around the inside of the dome declares, "You are Peter and on this rock I will build my church. To you I will give the keys of the kingdom of heaven." And directly beneath this dome—beneath the magnificent bronze altar canopy of Bernini, the current high altar, the successive medieval altars, the floor and foundations of Old St. Peter's, and the trophy mentioned by Caius—beneath all of this lies a poor man's grave that dates to the first century.

But is this really the grave of Peter himself?

Digging for Clues

It was only in the early twentieth century—an age when the Vatican authorities wanted to show that the Catholic Church was progressive and in touch with modern science—that extensive archaeological investigations were undertaken beneath the high altar at St. Peter's Basilica. Though professional archaeologists carried out the work, the project was supervised by a nonexpert: Monsignor Ludwig Kaas (1881–1952). A German priest and high-ranking politician whose capitulation to the Nazis in 1933 helped Adolf Hitler rise to power, Kaas was then exiled to a less dangerous position in the Vatican bureaucracy at Rome. After being put in charge of the physical structure of St. Peter's Basilica, he convinced his old friend Pope Pius XII to begin excavations of the ancient necropolis. It was this work that uncovered the trophy mentioned by Caius—and something else.

Unbeknownst to the archaeologists, Kaas would often come to the dig after hours, when everyone had gone home, and remove human bones for safekeeping. One night in 1942, with the help of a Vatican workman, Kaas took some bones from a marble-lined repository in a wall that was covered with ancient Christian graffiti about Peter. These human remains were placed in a wooden box and stored away. But when Kaas died in 1952, the box was forgotten by everyone except the workman whose probing hand had removed the relics.

Monsignor Kaas's successor as overseer of the excavations was a prominent archaeologist named Margherita Guarducci. One day in 1953, as she was standing at the graffiti wall beside the same worker who had emptied the repository more than a decade earlier, Guarducci wondered aloud what was once inside the cavity. The worker promptly led her to the wooden box and showed her the bones. However, because no one had originally considered these bones important, and because they had come from the wall repository instead of the ground itself, Guarducci assumed they must be from a later era.

Forensic work then focused on the bones from all the nearby graves; but disappointingly, the findings revealed that none of them could be Peter's. Another decade passed before the bones from the repository were finally subjected to scientific analysis. The results were truly remarkable: the wooden box contained the nearly complete (though badly decayed) skeleton of a robust human male who had died at an advanced age. These bones showed signs of once having been buried, then later being wrapped in a purple cloth with gold threads. At first, Guarducci dismissed the possibility that the relics could belong to Peter. Why were they not down in a grave? But then she remembered a chunk of the red wall, incised with graffiti, that had been found inside the cavity. In Guarducci's interpretation, the partial inscription read, "Peter is within."

What if Emperor Constantine's builders had placed the relics in the wall repository when the shrine was built for the new church—and then a worker had reached inside and scrawled an inscription into the adjoining wall so no one would forget? Excited, the esteemed archaeologist approached Pope Paul VI, informing him of her hypothesis. After further investigations, the final verdict of the Roman Catholic Church was announced to the world on June 26, 1968: the actual bones of St. Peter had been recovered! These relics, enclosed in transparent boxes, were replaced in the original repository in the graffiti wall, where they still remain today.

Whose Bones?

Are these the actual bones of the Prince of the Apostles? Due to a complex series of events since Peter's initial interment—including not only the confused circumstances surrounding Kaas and Guarducci but also the possible transfer of the relics to another catacomb for a short time in the third century, as well as the plundering of the basilica by Muslims in AD 846—we cannot be absolutely certain that the mysterious bones now lying beneath the high altar are those of Peter. We must also consider it somewhat strange that the bones would have been moved out of the original grave and into a nondescript hole in the wall. Although this would be more plausible if it were done to hide the precious relics during a time of persecution (rather than being the work of Constantine's builders, as Guarducci hypothesized), it still does not increase our confidence that we do, in fact, possess the actual bones today. Therefore, while the location of Peter's tomb is firmly established, the survival of his actual bones—though not impossible—is very much open to question.

UPON THIS ROCK

In this chapter we have given full attention to the textual and architectural clues about Peter's later life. Yet our lengthy journey has been worthwhile, if for no other reason than to catch a glimpse of how a simple Galilean fisherman was transformed into the first of 266 magnificent papal princes. The historical events surrounding the ancient figure of Peter affect all Christians today, even those who do not accept the supremacy of the Roman pontiff.

Although the words of Jesus to His leading disciple—"You are Peter, and on this rock I will build my church" (Matt. 16:18)—did not actually have the establishment of the papacy in view, the prediction was not simply meaningless. Jesus was saying something important here—not about Peter's faith, nor his verbal confession in verse 16, but clearly about Peter himself. The Lord identified His disciple *Petros* as the *petra*, or rock, of the church. Just because Catholic interpreters have built a massive edifice (both theologically and literally!) on this statement does not mean we should deny Jesus' obvious play on words.

So if Peter is indeed the rock of the church, in what sense is this true? We have no firm evidence that he thought of himself as a popelike figure, or even that he was in Rome for a substantial amount of time with a long-term ministry there. What we do know, both from the book of Acts as well as postbiblical tradition, is that Peter served as a cornerstone around which others could begin to build up the Christian faith. The content of his letters, the sermonic material recorded in Acts 2, and the substance of his gospel as captured by Mark all reveal Peter as the strong foundation of the church's first generation.

But let us remember, Peter didn't start out as a great hero. He was just a simple commoner trying to make a living until Jesus came along. Yet the same disciple who denied his Lord three times, declaring with curses and oaths, "I do not know the man" (Matt. 26:74), later offered the bold declaration to a Jerusalem crowd, "Let all the house of Israel therefore know for certain that God has made him both Lord and Christ, this Jesus whom you crucified" (Acts 2:36).

For clinging to this risky belief in the face of an emperor's tyranny, Peter was crucified on a Roman cross like his Master before him. It is the exaltation of the Lord Jesus Christ that Peter wanted to proclaim, in life as well as in death—and a watching world found that boldness irresistible. Who could have predicted that someone so ordinary would change history like this? Only God can take such feeble material and turn it into solid rock. Perhaps it was precisely this awareness of his own spiritual transformation that caused Peter to describe believers as "living stones . . . being built up as a spiritual house" (1 Peter 2:5). I, for one, am honored to be a brick in the mighty house that rests upon the labors of a Jewish fisherman named Petros.

REPORT CARD

PETER		
	Traveled widely on evangelistic missions	A
	Ministered in Rome and provided leadership for the Christians	A
	First arrived in Rome during the reign of Claudius (40s)	B
	Died by crucifixion in Nero's circus or surrounding gardens	A-
	Was crucified upside down	B
	Was buried in a grave now located beneath the altar of St. Peter's Basilica	A-
	Has had his bones recovered from inside the graffiti wall	B-
	Considered himself the preeminent authority figure of the Roman church	C-

A= Excellent, B= Good, C= Average, D= Below average, F= Not passing

CHAPTER 10

PAUL

The ministry of the apostle Paul was so powerful and pro-
ductive, it's easy to forget he was once a man "breathing
threats and murder" against the innocent (Acts 9:1). When the
martyr Stephen was stoned for his faith, Paul stood nearby and
approved the deed. Yet when Paul famously met the risen Christ
on the road to Damascus, he was transformed into a new person.
Now the very name he had persecuted became the content of his
gospel. For the remainder of his life—the next three decades—Paul
served his Lord as one of the boldest witnesses the church has ever
known. Indeed, the Christian religion would not exist in its present form without the life, ministry, and inspired writings of this
devoted evangelist.

A 180-degree turn like this is a classic part of many a great tale.
In fact, it's the stuff of which Hollywood blockbusters are made.
The outcast finds acceptance. The sinner finds redemption. The
pauper finds great riches. The wanderer finds his way. Only when
we see the protagonist make this dramatic turn and embark upon
a new road can the story be brought to a fitting conclusion.

It is somewhat strange, then, that in Paul's case, we do not know
exactly how our hero's story ends. Like the old Western movies,

the book of Acts concludes with Paul riding off into the sunset, having achieved his task of taking the gospel to the empire's capital. Yet such an ending isn't as satisfying as we might wish. The narrative trajectory that began on the Damascus road culminates with the church's foremost evangelist in chains for his faith in Rome. He has made his 180-degree turn . . . charted a new path . . . reached the world's greatest city. But then we are left wondering: What exactly happened to this great Christian figure after Acts?

PAUL IN ROME

Before we can assess the postbiblical traditions about the later life of Paul, we need to get a clear sense of where the scriptural story leaves him. Reconstructing the life of Paul is a difficult task involving numerous scholarly views on how to fit the chronology of the Pauline epistles into the framework provided in the book of Acts. Yet everyone agrees that Paul eventually came to Rome around AD 60. Luke relates in vivid detail how Paul and his companions were shipwrecked on the island of Malta before finally reaching the Italian coastline at Puteoli. This little harbor town—known today as Pozzuoli, a quaint suburb of the massive city of Naples—was once an important commercial port for the Alexandrian grain ships that fed the Italian people. Puteoli was connected to the southern road from Rome called the Via Appia, a major artery in the imperial road system. The route from Puteoli up the Appian Road was one of the main entry points for seafaring visitors from eastern lands traveling to Rome. Today the ancient road that Paul traveled as a chained prisoner buzzes with automobile traffic. Even so, it still runs past three early Christian burial complexes (the catacombs), through a gate in the old city walls, and into the city of Rome itself.

Paul's Roman Address

But once in Rome, where did Paul find lodging? Although the Bible does not provide us with his Roman address, a few tentative hypotheses can be offered. The historical evidence suggests that the first-century Christians were not spread evenly throughout the city but were clustered in specific areas.[1] Because they were primarily Greek-speaking immigrants of low socioeconomic status, they tended to congregate around the less desirable fringes of the city in unhealthy, low-lying slums.

One of the main Christian neighborhoods was the region around the gate through which the Appian Road passed, a region known for its impoverished laborers and numerous foreigners, including a large population of Jewish merchants and beggars.[2] However, the even more notable Jewish quarter was called Trans Tiberim because it was across the Tiber River from the walled city. Although today this is the trendy and artistic neighborhood of Trastevere, in ancient times the area was a squalid ghetto of poor immigrants and dockworkers. It was this busy, crowded place that many Jews—and the Christians after them—had decided to call home. In fact, the Trans Tiberim area was so well known for its Christian population that when the Great Fire of 64 burned most of Rome's regions to the ground, the inhabitants of this territory across the river—one of the few places the fire had spared—were punished as the obvious arsonists who must have started the blaze.

A very old tradition claims that the present-day church of San Paolo alla Regola (located near Trastevere) sits on the site of Paul's house arrest. While this cannot be known with certainty, it is reasonable to suggest Paul would have taken up residence near the Jewish community in order to evangelize his countrymen (Acts 28:17).

The area was also known for its leather tanneries, which might have allowed Paul to practice his trade of tent-making to pay for his lodging, as was his normal practice (Acts 18:3; 20:34). Therefore, we should imagine that Paul probably lived and worked in one of these two neighborhoods, with Trastevere being the more likely of the two. The apostle lived undisturbed in his own rented quarters and preached the gospel to Jews and Gentiles alike (Acts 28:16, 30-31). During this two-year period, he wrote his biblical epistles to the Ephesians, Philippians, Colossians, and Philemon. After this—at least according to Luke's historical story—the heroic Paul rode off into the sunset.

Yet just because Luke chose to end his narrative here doesn't mean we have to remain in the dark. Based on hints in some other biblical documents, as well as the reconstructed sources of ancient history and the testimonies of the church fathers, we are able to form a tentative answer to the question we can't help but ask: How did the apostle Paul's story turn out in the end?

PLANS FOR SPAIN

We know that Paul not only wished to visit Spain, he fully intended to go there. In AD 57, he wrote ahead to the Roman church and declared, "I hope to see you in passing as I go to Spain, and to be helped on my journey there by you, once I have enjoyed your company for a while" (Rom. 15:24). Then, after describing the financial donation he has collected for the Jerusalem saints, Paul once again asserts, "When therefore I have completed this and have delivered to them what has been collected, I will leave for Spain by way of you" (v. 28). Notice that in Paul's mind, the Roman Christians were merely a stop along the way. His real destination was Spain! Paul planned to go there after passing through Rome to receive spiritual and material assistance from the brethren.

The Iberian Peninsula (modern Spain and Portugal) had begun to be colonized by the Romans as early as the 200s BC. By Paul's day, the territory of Hispania was very Romanized, having thoroughly embraced its new identity as part of the empire. And it wasn't actually very far from the capital. The Roman statesman and naturalist Pliny the Elder asserted that the farthermost part of Hispania could be reached by sea in seven days from Rome's port, while the nearer part of Spain would take only four days.[3] For a veteran traveler like Paul, a four-day sea voyage would have been a breeze. There is no reason why someone as doggedly determined as Paul could not have made this trip out of Rome. All it would take is a little money and a release from his house arrest—which is probably what happened when his Jewish accusers from the east failed to show up in the capital to press their charges (see Acts 28:21).

To the Ends of the World

But why Spain? Although Paul didn't offer a precise reason for his steadfast intent to go there, the symbolism of that country in the Greco-Roman mindset may give us a clue. The ancients viewed Spain as the farthest end of the world. Like most people in Europe until the time of Christopher Columbus, the Romans considered the Atlantic Ocean to stretch away from Spain's western coast into the vast unknown. Based on this common cultural perspective, Paul seems to have invested the provinces of Hispania with cosmic significance: they symbolized the outer boundary of the world he was trying to reach with the gospel.

In Romans 15:16–21, Paul declares his life's calling as a missionary to the unreached. He expresses his intent to evangelize "not where Christ has already been named, lest I build on someone else's foundation, but as it is written, 'Those who have never been told of him will see, and those who have never heard will understand'" (vv. 20–21; see also Acts 13:47). To fulfill these words, Paul realized he would have to visit the area that was universally acknowledged as the empire's western boundary in the Mediterranean: Hispania, the land beyond which nothing existed but empty sea.

The Old Testament had even predicted the rise of this great evangelistic work. In Isaiah 66:19, God declares that His glory will one day be known among all the nations—even at Tarshish, a place associated with "the coastlands far away, that have not heard my fame or seen my glory" (see also Ps. 72:8–10 and Jonah 1:3, where Tarshish likewise represents the uttermost ends of the earth). The biblical city of Tarshish is sometimes equated with the ancient civilization of Tartessos on the Atlantic coast of Spain. Although this equation cannot be absolutely proven, Paul does seem to have thought of Spain as his own equivalent of Tarshish, the distant land as far to the west as anyone can go. Therefore he viewed his journey to Spain as part of God's plan to bring the saving knowledge of Jesus Christ to all the nations of the world.

Paul points out in Romans 15:19 that he has already evangelized from Jerusalem to the edge of Italy. Now he intends to enter Italy, and from there reach the end of the world. Apparently the Spanish mission held great symbolic value to this globally minded apostle.

The Extremities of the West

Very early testimony from the ancient church suggests Paul did in fact reach Spain. The Christian bishop Clement of Rome states, "After preaching both in the east and west, [Paul] gained the illustrious reputation due to his faith, having taught righteousness to the whole world, and come to the extreme limit of the west, and suffered martyrdom under the prefects" (ANF, vol. 1, *First Epistle of Clement* 5).[4] Clement's terms "the whole world" and "the extreme limit of the west" can only refer to Spain, for it is exactly how someone writing from Rome in the late first century would have referred to the westernmost edge of his known world.

Later church traditions agree with Clement's assertion that Paul reached Spain. In the *Acts of Peter*, compiled in the late second century from earlier stories, we read, "And after Paul had fasted three days and asked of the Lord that which should be profitable for him, he saw a vision, even the Lord saying unto him: 'Arise, Paul, and become a physician [by going in person] to them that are in Spain.'"[5] In this story, all the Roman Christians accompany Paul to the harbor and bid him a sad farewell as he departs for the west. Likewise, the canon list called the Muratorian Fragment mentions "the journey of Paul, when he went from the city—Rome—to Spain" (ANF, vol. 5, Caius, *Canon Muratorianus*).

After this, many church fathers such as Jerome, Athanasius, and John Chrysostom agree that Paul went to Spain. Of course, we need not assume he traveled all the way past the Strait of Gibraltar and out into the Atlantic. The Mediterranean city of Tarraco (modern Tarragona), an important imperial capital in one of the Spanish provinces, was only a four-day sail from Rome. Paul probably came here for a short time and tried to establish a church, yet met with little success. This would explain why no detailed account of his work in Spain is recorded, or even imagined, by the earliest Christian chroniclers.

IMPRISONED ONCE MORE

If Paul's Spanish initiative was short-lived, we are faced with the question of what he did next. At this point, some historians will turn to biblical evidence to fill in the gaps, while others will not. According to conservative scholars, the Pastoral Epistles (i.e., 1 and 2 Timothy and Titus) are just what they present themselves to be—letters penned by the apostle Paul himself. Liberal scholars, on the other hand, view the Pastorals as being written by a later author using Paul's name to extend his ideas to the next generation. Therefore, it is only biblical conservatives who will use the circumstances behind the composition of the Pastoral Epistles as valid evidence for Paul's whereabouts after being released from prison.[6]

But even if we accept the conservative position, we are still left in the dark when it comes to the details about these years. Only a few basic outlines emerge. Paul wrote his first epistle to Timothy while his younger protégé was ministering at Ephesus; and Titus had been left by Paul on the island of Crete when he received his own epistle. Therefore, after Paul's abortive trip to Spain, it seems he returned to the Aegean Sea region he knew so well. There he became reacquainted with the issues facing the eastern churches, prompting him to write letters to two key pastors with instructions about how to govern their respective congregations. However, exactly when or from where Paul wrote these letters cannot be determined.

A Letter from Prison

What about 2 Timothy? This letter is important for our purposes because it depicts Paul enduring an arduous confinement. Unlike his former house arrest in which he was fairly comfortable and possessed a measure of freedom, Paul is now clearly suffering. Feeling alone and abandoned, the great apostle laments, "Luke alone is with me" (2 Tim. 4:11). He then expresses his desire for further companionship by urging Timothy to "get Mark and bring him with you, for he is very useful to me for ministry." Paul also grieves that all the Asian Christians have rejected him except Onesiphorus, who came to Rome and diligently sought the obscure place where Paul was imprisoned, until at last he found his friend (2 Tim. 1:15–18).

Yet even with this encouragement, Paul's awareness of his imminent death cannot be suppressed. "I am already being poured out as a drink offering," he declares, "and the time of my departure has come. I have fought the good fight, I have finished the race, I have kept the faith. Henceforth there is laid up for me the crown of righteousness, which the Lord, the righteous judge, will award to me on that Day" (2 Tim. 4:6–8). The profound emotions expressed here—both sad and hopeful at once—have prompted many observers of church history to seek the very place from which they were written.

In Which Dungeon?

One of the most famous places associated with early Christianity in Rome is the so-called Mamertine Prison. According to late traditions of unknown origin, both Peter and Paul were imprisoned in this dungeon situated on the Roman forum next to the Senate house. It is said that when two of the apostles' jailers, Processus and Martinian, were converted to the true faith, a miracle caused water to spring up in the prison's underground cell so Peter could carry out the rite of baptism. Could this be the actual place from which the apostle Paul wrote his final letter to Timothy?

Unfortunately, though the Mamertine Prison can still be visited today as a gaudy tourist attraction, there is no good reason to think it was ever truly associated with either Peter or Paul. These legends appear to have originated no earlier than the seventh century, a time when apostolic and martyrological mythmaking was in full swing. While the Mamertine Prison (originally known as the Tullianum) was indeed used for important political prisoners, it probably would not have housed two no-names like Peter and Paul. The precise place in Rome where Paul mournfully composed 2 Timothy remains unknowable to us today.

Yet compose it he did, and from an oppressive Roman dungeon. How exactly did Paul wind up in Rome enduring this harsh second imprisonment? Many commentators suggest he was rearrested for his evangelistic activities in the provinces. This is certainly possible. However, without the influence of the accusers who had so ardently opposed him in Jerusalem, we must wonder why the Roman authorities in a completely different region from where Paul was originally arrested would jump-start the proceedings against him again. Would they have even known about this case? It's not as if they would have had access to a database of all crimes in the vast empire. After a two-year house arrest followed by an unknown period of subsequent ministry, the proceedings against Paul would have been long forgotten outside of Rome.

Who then would have put this obscure Jew back in chains and remanded him to the custody of the supreme court? An answer is not forthcoming. Therefore, we must at least consider the hypothesis that Paul returned of his own volition to the imperial capital, where he immediately found himself in the crosshairs of Emperor Nero, one of the most tyrannical, vicious, and paranoid emperors ever to rule over Rome.

PAUL AND NERO

As we grapple with the historical thesis that Paul was arrested and executed under Nero, we need to take a look at the precise crime with which the apostle would have been charged. The book of Acts describes how the Jewish leaders from Jerusalem vehemently opposed Paul's views about the law of Moses. However, this would have mattered very little to the imperial authorities, for it was not a topic about which Roman jurisprudence was concerned

(Acts 25:18). So what crime could have gotten Paul thrown in jail—first in Jerusalem, then Caesarea, then finally in Rome?

Originally the problem was a disturbance of the peace resulting from Paul's theological claims (Acts 21:27–36). This was enough to get Paul arrested. Yet as the trial proceeded over many months and the judges seemed to be favoring the Jews, Paul sensed the situation turning against him. He determined his best legal strategy was an appeal to Caesar—that is, to Emperor Nero. The judge's response was quick and emphatic: "To Caesar you have appealed; to Caesar you shall go" (Acts 25:12).

Nero the Madman

By all accounts, the man to whom Paul had appealed was a depraved lunatic. As the adopted son of the former emperor Claudius, Nero came to power in AD 54 at the age of seventeen. For a while his reign was peaceful. But after murdering his mother in 59, Nero embarked on a downward spiral of sexual debauchery and paranoid madness that ultimately led to his death as an enemy of the state. One of Nero's special obsessions was the perception of his imperial majesty, which made him exceptionally vain and hypersensitive to even the tiniest hint of disrespect. He insisted on being called "lord" and "savior," and he was given religious honors as a divinity. The Roman crime of treason, originally involving acts of military betrayal or assistance to foreign enemies, came to include any threat to the emperor's right to rule. Therefore, the Christians' claim to follow another Lord and Savior who would soon usher in a glorious new kingdom quickly aroused Nero's concern.

Paul's Army?

The early church texts that tell the story of Paul's martyrdom provide evidence of precisely this sort of political paranoia on the part of Nero. As we have already seen with the other apostles, a collection of traditional stories about Paul circulated among various groups of believers in the second century. These free-floating stories were edited into a single narrative called the *Acts of Paul* prior to AD 200. Interestingly, much of the book's plot centers not on the apostle himself but his most devoted female disciple, a young beauty named Thecla who abandons her intended marriage in order to follow Paul and minister at his side. While this tale exhibits a high degree of fanciful imagination, the independent textual unit that described Paul's martyrdom contains some important hints about Nero. At one point, we read that Nero's cupbearer Patroclus was reported to have died; but unbeknownst to the emperor, he was healed by Paul through the power of Christ. When Nero is then startled to find his cupbearer standing before him unharmed, the following exchange takes place:

Patroclus, livest thou?

And he said: I live, Caesar.

And he said: Who is he that made thee to live?

And the lad, full of the mind of faith, said: Christ Jesus, the king of the ages.

And Caesar was troubled and said: Shall he, then, be king of the ages and overthrow all kingdoms?

Patroclus saith unto him: Yea, he overthroweth all kingdoms and he alone shall be for ever, and there shall be no kingdom that shall escape him.

And he smote him on the face and said: Patroclus, art thou also a soldier of that king?

And he said: Yea, Lord Caesar, for he raised me when I was dead.[7]

A little later in this text, after Paul has been brought forward to testify before Nero, the emperor demands to know why Paul is raising an army of Christian soldiers in lands belonging to Rome. Paul boldly replies that he serves a King who has soldiers everywhere—not just within the Roman Empire but throughout the world. Nero is invited to serve and bow to this universal king; yet if he will not, he should know that the day is soon coming when Jesus will judge the whole world with fire. "And when Caesar heard that," the *Acts of Paul* relates, "he commanded all the

[Christian] prisoners to be burned with fire, but Paul to be beheaded after the law of the Romans." Clearly, the ancient believers who enjoyed these thrilling stories considered Paul's martyrdom to stem from treasonous behavior toward the empire's supreme ruler.[8]

Charges Dropped

In all probability, then, the official charge lodged against Paul when he was first taken to Rome in chains was injury to the imperial majesty. Although a local disturbance of the peace had initiated the judicial process, only something as grievous as treason would have been sufficient to require sending the prisoner to the capital.

Yet without anyone to press charges against him, the case was dropped after the required two-year waiting period had elapsed. No one from Jerusalem was willing to come to Rome and continue the accusation, so Paul was released. Being an official Roman citizen probably helped Paul here. Not only did citizens possess legal protections that the masses did not enjoy, but the imperial court in Rome also would have been more favorable to such a high-ranking person than to a group of Jews from a distant province who wanted to wrangle about theology.

Even so, Paul was in a dangerous situation, for the crime of treason was always taken seriously. Though the charges were dropped for lack of an accuser, Paul was still on record as a potential threat to the emperor. And as it turns out, we have good reason to believe Nero eventually did become aware of this lurking threat to his reign.

Did Paul Appear Before Nero?

In Acts 27:24, Paul describes the angelic vision he received during the storm at sea that wrecked his ship and cast him adrift. "Do not be afraid, Paul," the angel commanded. "You must stand before Caesar. And behold, God has granted you all those who sail with you." Yet despite this prediction of a trial before Nero, we have already seen that when Paul arrived in Rome, he was kept under house arrest for two years without ever being tried.

But later, while enduring his second, more difficult, imprisonment, Paul laments, "At my first defense no one came to stand by me, but all deserted me" (2 Tim. 4:16). Since no trial is recorded during Paul's first detention in Acts 28, nor does he seem to be entirely abandoned at that point, the statement here probably refers to a preliminary hearing before the imperial court during the second Pauline imprisonment. Although this initial inquest may not have included the emperor himself, it would not be surprising if at some point Nero summoned Paul and heard his case firsthand.

The historical sources tell us that Nero did not try as many judicial cases as his predecessors. Nevertheless, the one thing that always commanded his attention was a threat to his imperial majesty. In the previous chapter on Peter, we learned how, according to the historian Tacitus, Nero tried to pin the blame for the Great Fire of 64 on the Christians. Persecution of the church is also attested by the ancient historian Suetonius, who records that Nero "inflicted punishments on the Christians, a sort of people who held a new and impious superstition."[9] Thus we learn from two different historical sources that Nero not only knew about Christianity but despised it.

Where would he have learned about this religion? Admittedly, he could have gained information through his advisers. Yet why would this paranoid emperor not take an hour to hear from a Roman citizen who had been brought before his court, a prominent Christian leader who could inform him more directly about this new threat to his imperial majesty? The idea is entirely reasonable; and in light of the angel's words in Acts 27:24, we can suppose it may well have happened.

Reconstructing the Timeline

But exactly when, and under what circumstances, would this trial before Nero have taken place? Perhaps we can reconstruct the chronology of Paul's final years like this. After being released from house arrest in AD 62, he attempted to start a church in Spain but met with little success. By the spring of 63 he was back in the region around the Aegean Sea,[10] heavily involved once more with the fledgling house churches of Asia Minor, Greece, and Crete. While it is possible that these ministry activities got Paul rearrested, we have no good reason to think any local officials would have had the motivation to apprehend him, much less send him back to the emperor's court in Rome. It seems more reasonable to suggest that Paul returned to Rome of his own volition.

Why? One plausible reason could be the devastating citywide fire of 64. Concerned for the welfare of the flock in Rome, Paul hurried to the capital, perhaps even bringing financial contributions to provide much-needed charity for the brothers and sisters there. In support of this argument, we can note that the fourth-century church historian Eusebius does not say Paul was brought to Rome by force. Eusebius merely states that "after he had made his defense,[11] it is said that the apostle was sent again upon the ministry of preaching, and that upon coming to the same city a second time, he suffered martyrdom. In this imprisonment he wrote his second epistle to Timothy, in which he mentions his first defense and his impending death" (NPNF2, vol. 1, *C.H.* 2.22.2). Eusebius's expression "upon coming to the same city" implies that the journey was an action Paul undertook freely. The verb itself conveys the sense of a mere arrival, without any overtones of being forced or compelled. Therefore, the hypothesis of a rearrest in the provinces is not as likely as a voluntary trip to Rome.

The Sentence Comes Down

However, the world into which the apostle now stepped had been thrown into chaos. Nero had grown far more unstable since Paul's first sojourn in the city. Blame was being cast everywhere for the inferno—and since the primary Christian region of Trans Tiberim had been left unscathed by the flames, both the populace and the imperial authorities were asking hard questions. In this context, we can imagine that a few of the church's recognized leaders were arrested and questioned. It wouldn't have taken much investigation to learn that the Christians' primary allegiance was not to the divine emperor but the true Lord of the cosmos.

Peter—a commoner with no legal protections—was immediately subjected to the hideous torments that Nero devised for the Christians in his circus on the Vatican Field. Paul, on the other hand, was a Roman citizen. His trial on charges of injury to the emperor's majesty would have proceeded according to the dictates of Roman law. Yet the groundwork for Paul's execution had already been laid during his previous detention. He was clearly a troublemaker from the east who held no regard for the ancient gods of Rome—a thing demanded of every true citizen. It should come as no surprise, then, that around AD 65 or 66, Paul was found guilty of the crime of treason.[12]

MARTYRDOM

From ancient Rome to the United States today, treason has normally been considered a crime punishable by death. Therefore when Paul was convicted of injury to the emperor's majesty, his fate was sealed. As a Roman citizen, he would not have been crucified or thrown to wild beasts in the arena but given the more humane penalty of death by decapitation. Judicial actions like this typically occurred outside the city walls along a main road near a gate. A special executioner called a *speculator* (originally a field scout, but later a high-ranking staff officer of the emperor's bodyguard) carried out the sentence by severing the condemned's head.

The weapon used for this purpose was normally a sword, not an axe. Many accounts of the martyrs refer to "swords" as the instrument of punishment. For example, the famous Christian noblewoman Perpetua guided the gladiator's sword to her throat (ANF, vol. 3, *Passion of the Holy Martyrs Perpetua and Felicitas* 6.4); and when the Roman governor of Africa sentenced some other martyrs to death, he declared that since they "obstinately persisted" in remaining Christians, "it is determined that they be put to the sword" (ANF, vol. 9, *Passion of the Scillitan Martyrs*). Ever since the Middle Ages, Paul has been depicted in Christian art holding a sword, the emblem of his death. Church tradition is probably correct about this. But what else can we determine about his execution?

Acts of Paul

Since Luke did not tell his readers how Paul's story turned out in the book of Acts, the early Christians decided to fill in the gap. That is why the work we mentioned above called the *Acts of Paul*—and indeed, the entire genre of the "apocryphal acts of the apostles"—developed so quickly and enjoyed such widespread popularity in the ancient church. The *Acts of Paul* should not really be viewed as a single document, but a series of intertwined stories composed in, or translated into, various languages over several centuries. The earliest version goes back to the second century, and for that reason it is the most reliable of all the different accounts. Though it is full of fantastic legends and heroic episodes in the life of Paul, the martyrdom narrative probably preserves an accurate historical core of a trial before Nero's court. As we have seen, the text recounts how Paul confronted Nero with bold predictions of imminent judgment, which infuriated the vain emperor. In light of the known personalities of both of these men, an event like this certainly could have happened in a volatile courtroom.

Then the *Acts of Paul* recounts how Nero went through Rome executing Christians without a trial, until the people finally demanded an end to the bloodshed. This remembrance can likewise be considered reliable because it is paralleled in the record preserved by the pagan historian Tacitus, who remarked that while everyone in Rome agreed the Christians deserved punishment, "there arose a sentiment of pity, due to the impression that they were being sacrificed not for the welfare of the state but to the ferocity of a single man."[13]

The *Acts of Paul* goes on to describe the apostle's prediction that he will appear alive to Nero after his execution. Paul then evangelizes two Roman officials, to whom he promises to send Titus and Luke with the offer of Christian baptism. At last Paul is brought to the place of his punishment:

> Then Paul stood with his face to the east and lifted up his hands unto heaven and prayed a long time, and in his prayer he conversed in the Hebrew tongue with the fathers, and then stretched forth his neck without speaking. And when the executioner (speculator) struck off his head, milk spurted upon the cloak of the soldier. And the soldier and all that were there present, when they saw it, marveled and glorified God [who] had given such glory unto Paul: and they went and told Caesar what was done.[14]

Of course, after his death, Paul makes good on his promise to appear to Nero, which so frightens the emperor that he releases all the Christians from jail and ends the persecution against the church. Then Titus and Luke do indeed baptize[15] the two Roman officials, and the story closes with a final benediction. Obviously, there is a legendary ring to the *Acts of Paul*. Can we find any corroboration of its details elsewhere?

Other Accounts

Other writers of the ancient church, though not delving into as much narrative detail as the *Acts of Paul*, nonetheless provide further evidence that Paul was martyred at Rome. We have already seen that the local bishop Clement made this claim in the late first century. Similarly, Ignatius of Antioch (early second century) wrote on the way to his martyrdom that he would soon be following in Paul's footsteps (ANF, vol. 1, *To the Ephesians* 12). Bishop Polycarp (early- to mid-second century) likewise included Paul among those who have suffered for Christ (ANF, vol. 1, *To the Philippians* 9).

Around 200, Tertullian declared that Rome was the place where "Peter endures a passion like his Lord's, where Paul wins his crown in a death like John's" (ANF, vol. 3, *Prescription Against Heretics* 36). This is clearly a reference to Peter's crucifixion like Jesus, and Paul's decapitation like John the Baptist. From this time on, everyone accepted the tradition of Paul's martyrdom at Rome. We find it mentioned in Lactantius, Eusebius, John Chrysostom, Jerome, and Augustine. A late fourth-century coffin even depicts the scene visually: a stern-looking soldier draws his sword as he approaches the bound apostle, who is standing in the reedy swampland next to the Tiber River. After this, many other coffins copied the same scene. It was the universal belief of the Christian church from a very early time that Paul died as a martyr under Nero. No other competing tradition has ever emerged.

The Ostian Road

Where exactly did the execution take place? The earliest records agree that Paul was beheaded on the road leading southwest from Rome toward its seaport—that is, the Ostian Road, which ran nineteen miles from the city to the mouth of the Tiber on the coast. The most important reference to this location is preserved for us by Eusebius in the fourth century, but it reproduces the testimony of a much earlier church leader at Rome named Caius.

In our chapter on Peter, we discovered that Caius (sometimes called Gaius) had bragged about his city: "And I can show the trophies of the apostles. For if you choose to go to the Vatican or to the Ostian Road, you will find the trophies of those who founded this church" (ANF, vol. 5, *Fragments of Caius*). This evidence tells us that no later than 200, a "trophy" existed on the Ostian Road to memorialize the death of Paul. Most scholars understand this edifice to be a tomb near the spot where Paul was martyred, for Eusebius declares that the trophies were "the places where the sacred corpses of the aforesaid apostles are laid" (NPNF2, vol. 1, *C.H.* 2.25.6). A fourth-century calendar called the *Burying of the*

Martyrs also identifies the place of Paul's martyrdom as the Ostian Road. But do we know the exact site?

A Church to Mark the Trophy

When Emperor Constantine came to power in the early 300s, he began to subsidize a church building program. He donated a cathedral in Rome for the bishop (now known as the Archbasilica of St. John Lateran), and he also had a role in sponsoring Old St. Peter's. In addition to this, the architects of Constantine's era constructed a small chapel on the Ostian Road over what they understood to be the trophy of Paul's grave. Archaeology has confirmed that at the time of the apostle's death, this site was located within a Roman burial ground that lay just outside the city.

Within a few decades, however, it became apparent that this little chapel was insufficient to serve the many pilgrims who were flocking to pray at Paul's tomb. In 384, Emperor Theodosius, along with his two co-emperors, wrote to the mayor of Rome and expressed his intent to erect a new church on the site. This building was to be much more magnificent, with lavish decorations and plenty of space for visitors. In fact, when it was completed, it was even larger than the church of St. Peter. A wide avenue was constructed to provide access to the impressive building with unhindered views, making it a major suburban landmark on the Ostian Road. Soon a triumphal arch was added to the church directly over the tomb. In honor of the pious donations of two Roman emperors, the arch's mosaic inscription declared, "Theodosius began and Honorius finished this hall, which is sanctified by the body of Paul, the teacher of the world." At last the apostle Paul had a shrine worthy of his stature in church history.

Over the next fourteen centuries, the church atop the Pauline trophy remained essentially intact, even as other Roman churches fell into disrepair and were razed, or were entirely remodeled according to later architectural tastes. But in 1823, disaster finally struck: a workman repairing the roof started a fire that burned most of the structure to the ground. Yet in the process of rebuilding the splendid church that can be visited today, an interesting artifact came to light.

It was discovered that in ancient times, the original trophy of Paul had been encased in a monument whose marble slabs were marked with the dedicatory inscription, "To Paul, the apostle and martyr." Later these plaques were affixed to the top of the monument, and holes were bored through them so libations could be poured into the tomb, or cloths could be lowered to sit next to the holy bones until they had achieved healing power.[16]

Then in 2002, Vatican excavations beneath the altar uncovered a stone sarcophagus dating to the time when the second basilica was erected by Theodosius and his son Honorius. This coffin, though surrounded by several layers of later construction, had remained in its initial position, unmoved and unmolested since the late fourth century. The archaeologists concluded that the contents of the original tomb had been moved into this sarcophagus when the Theodosian church was built. In confirmation of this, Pope Benedict XVI announced in 2009 that scientific investigations inside the coffin had revealed human bone fragments that dated to the first or second century. "This seems to confirm the unanimous and uncontested tradition that they are the mortal remains of the apostle Paul," the pope declared.

And because this spot has been continuously revered as Paul's tomb since very ancient times, it may well be true. Visitors to the church of St. Paul Outside the Walls have good reason to believe the apostle's body actually does rest inside the sarcophagus that can be viewed through a grate beneath the altar.

Other Traditions

Of course, rival traditions have cropped up through the years. One story relates that the true location of Paul's martyrdom was a little farther down the road from his burial site. When Paul's severed head hit the ground, it bounced three times as it uttered the words "Jesus, Jesus, Jesus," which caused three springs of water to well up. Today the church of St. Paul at the Three Fountains marks that very spot—but it is clearly the result of later legends that carry no historical validity.[17]

In contrast, a more authentic site of Pauline veneration was the original burial ground that gave us the word "catacomb." The Greek expression *kata kymbas* means "down in the bowls," which was a colloquial way that the early Christians referred to a quarry pit on the Appian Road where they had begun to bury their dead in the third century. Certain church documents refer to the remains of Peter and Paul being temporarily transferred here during a major persecution. Commemorative banquets for these glorious martyrs were celebrated by devout Christians in an open-air dining room at the cemetery, and even today the diners' prayers to the apostles can still be seen at the Catacombs of St. Sebastian, scratched into the walls as graffiti. However, many scholars doubt the holy relics were actually moved here for a time—and even if they were, no connection to either Peter or Paul can be established at this location prior to the third century. It certainly was not the original grave site of either of these apostles.

The best church traditions, then, suggest that Paul was buried right where he was martyred: on the Ostian Road at the spot where the Basilica of St. Paul Outside the Walls now stands. Among this church's many decorations is a beautiful wooden door inlaid with bronze panels designed by the Italian sculptor Guido Veroi in 2008. The panels depict several important scenes from Paul's life, including his conversion and martyrdom on two distinct roadsides. But perhaps the most poignant image of all is the Bible verse that the door records in both Greek and Latin: "It is no longer I who live, but Christ who lives in me" (Gal. 2:20). These ringing words, more than any physical church or monument, reflect the deepest desire of the apostle Paul. To be filled with the presence of his Lord and Savior is the only way he wanted his story to end.

REPORT CARD

PAUL

Was released from his first Roman imprisonment	A
Went on a mission trip to Spain	B
Ministered in the Aegean after his release	A
Was imprisoned in the Mamertine	C
Was tried before Nero himself	A-
Was convicted of treason and executed on the Ostian Road	A
Was beheaded at the "Three Fountains"	D-
Is still buried at St. Paul Outside the Walls	B+

A= Excellent, B= Good, C= Average, D= Below average, F= Not passing

CONCLUSION

The question that lies at the heart of this book—"What happened to the apostles after Acts?"—is compelling to any Christian who loves the characters that populate the pages of Scripture. Because we encounter the beginnings of the apostolic stories in the Bible yet rarely reach their finales, our natural response is to wonder how things turned out. We want to know more about our biblical heroes. This book has tried to fill in those gaps from a historian's point of view. Along the way, we have learned as much as we possibly can about the primary leaders of the New Testament church.

Does this mean, then, that the story is now complete? In the words of the apostle Paul, "May it never be!" The saga of church history didn't end with the last verse of Acts. It kept on rolling right up to our own day.

Too often we imagine that God's story came to a screeching halt at the end of the apostolic period, or maybe that it fizzled in the second generation. Certainly by the time of Emperor Constantine, it is understood to have met with great disaster. This common viewpoint has caused many Christians to function with a "big ditch" view of church history: that the space between the pristine period of the apostles and the Protestant Reformation is a vast wasteland. But is that true? No. God did not abandon His church in the second century, nor in the fourth, nor even in the fifteenth. All of church history belongs to the believer today—the good, the bad, and the ugly.

My purpose in writing a book on the apostles has not been to glamorize the first generation of believers at the expense of all the rest. Just the opposite: I have tried to set the apostles into the context of the later church fathers who received, admired, remembered—and sometimes distorted!—the founding figures of the Christian faith. In this way I hope that my book will serve as an entrance into the broader world of the ancient church.

If you wish to read more about this period, I have written a work that I intended as a primer for the curious Christian: *Getting to Know the Church Fathers: An Evangelical Introduction* (Brazos, 2007; second edition forthcoming from Baker Academic). I have also written a book about the faithful confessors who paid the ultimate price for Jesus: *Early Christian Martyr Stories: An Evangelical Introduction with New Translations* (Baker Academic, 2014). I suggest these books to you, not to build up my own ego but because I truly believe in what they have to offer the body of Christ. Whether you read these books or one of the many excellent introductions out there, my prayer is that in some fashion you will begin to explore the ancient contours of your faith.

So then, what happened to the apostles after Acts? The answer is simple. They died and went on to their reward—but they also left behind their successors, the men and women who received the torch of the Christian faith and passed it to the next generation.

This process continued through the centuries. Now the torch has come down to us. What will we do with it? Wisdom would suggest that we learn from our forebears how to lift high the sacred flame. It has been well kept by those who have finished the race and are watching us compete. May we too be marked by courage and perseverance as we run the race set before us . . . because the One who is waiting for us at the end is entirely worth it.

NOTES

Introduction:

1. Scholars also debate whether Romans 16:7 refers to Andronicus and Junia as apostles, but in the present book I follow the ESV translation in which they are not designated as such.

2. This academic field used to be known as *patristics*, or the study of the ancient church fathers (from Latin *pater*, father). However, because that term has come to be viewed by many scholars as too masculine and religious, it has fallen out of favor. The more common designation these days is *early Christian studies*.

3. This viewpoint came from a German theologian named Walter Bauer, who wrote *Orthodoxy and Heresy in Earliest Christianity* (1934). Though Bauer is now deceased, some very fine scholars still hold to a version of his so-called Bauer Thesis. One of the most notable advocates of this view today is Bart Ehrman. See his *Lost Christianities* (2005).

4. History.hanover.edu/texts/trent.html, Council of Trent, Fourth Session, 18.

5. Vatican.va/archive/index.htm, II Vatican Council, *Dei Verbum* 24; see also 9.

6. Some readers may be familiar with the term Apocrypha as a designation for the extra Old Testament books that appear in Catholic Bibles. These are Jewish documents preserved in Greek from the time between the Old and New Testaments—which means they are non-Christian texts composed primarily during the BC period. Despite the similar name, the "New Testament apocrypha" are an entirely different body of writings: Christian works that cropped up in the early church to expand on the stories found in the New Testament. Since

these works did not carry the same authority as the original apostolic writings—and sometimes even verged close to heresy—they came to be called *apocrypha*, that is, hidden works that had been withdrawn from public use in the church. As the canon of Scripture came together and solidified in the fourth century, works that formerly had been read aloud in church ceased to have that function.

Chapter 1: Matthew

1. The NPNF edition reads "everyone *interpreted* them as he was able," but the original Greek verb probably meant *translated* in this context.

2. A minority of scholars, both liberal and conservative, believes these two gospels were not independent but that Luke used Matthew as a source. I recognize the validity of this argument, but in this book I take the predominant scholarly view that Mark and Q were independently used by Matthew and Luke.

3. "Jewish-Christians" were ethnic Jews who had accepted Jesus yet continued to emphasize Old Testament themes, practices, and prophecies. The Jewishness of Jesus the Messiah was highlighted in such communities. See chapter 7 on James for more about Jewish-Christians.

4. For example, of the four gospels, only Matthew records the remark of Jesus about a king's troops sacking and burning Jerusalem (22:7). Perhaps an editor added this remembrance after AD 70 to remind the church that Jesus knew all along this was going to happen. The gospel of Matthew also includes a statement by Jesus that has a distinct Trinitarian ring to it (28:19). The choice to include this saying of the Lord could reflect the theological interests of a later time when baptism in the threefold name had become standard in the church.

Chapter 2: Mark

1. I have supplied the names in this passage because Eusebius's use of pronouns is sometimes confusing.

2. For a more confident assessment than mine concerning Mark's likely presence in Alexandria, see the recent work of the excellent scholar Thomas C. Oden: *The African Memory of Mark: Reassessing Early Church Tradition* (InterVarsity, 2011). Unfortunately, I cannot accept the author's methodology in which he gives credence to very late sources that supposedly preserve "African memory." There is no guarantee these "memories" actually correspond to historical reality. They are more likely to be—like so many traditional texts—based on rumors and legends from centuries after the fact. I believe we must view such texts with a more critical eye.

3. Stephen C. Carlson, *The Gospel Hoax: Morton Smith's Invention of Secret Mark* (Waco, TX: Baylor University Press, 2005), 62–63.

Chapter 3: Luke

1. Historical analysis of the list of names in Romans 16 suggests most of the believers in the capital city were of low socioeconomic status. However, Luke's medical background indicates he was likely to have been a literate man of higher social standing, and he may even have received an excellent classical education. Such a person would be a good candidate to author a work like Luke–Acts, which displays an elegant Greek style and an awareness of the conventions of cultured historiography. For further information on the subject of early Christian literacy, see the work of my former professor Harry Y. Gamble, *Books and Readers in the Early Church: A History of Early Christian Texts* (New Haven, CT: Yale University Press, 1997).

Chapter 4: John

1. Some scholars doubt Polycarp actually knew the apostle John, but I do not think this connection is as dubious as they suggest. It is chronologically and geographically possible, and it is attested in other sources. Yet even if it is inaccurate, Polycarp certainly moved in the circles of those who revered John. Irenaeus could have gained accurate information about the apostle from this source even if he were mistaken about the direct relationship between the two men.

2. The two still-living men are explicitly said to be "disciples of the Lord." This can only refer to the apostle John and another figure whom Papias knew, a man by the name of Aristion. We have no other knowledge of Aristion, but perhaps he could have been one of Jesus' seventy-two (Luke 10:1) or five hundred (1 Cor. 15:6) original followers. There is every reason to expect that at least a few of these five hundred-plus individuals would have been known to Papias. Thus, both Aristion and the apostle John can be considered "disciples of the Lord."

3. Two of these references are, however, attributed to Papias, which would make them more trustworthy; but historians are not certain about this attribution. Even if it were valid, the predominant church tradition about John is that he lived into old age and died peacefully. This also seems to be the implication of John 21:20–22, which records the disciples' belief that John would live for a long time.

Chapter 5: Mary

1. Note, however, that the original Protestant, Martin Luther, *did* believe in the perpetual virginity of Mary, and in fact he maintained a robust veneration of the Blessed Virgin throughout his life. Other early Protestants like Ulrich Zwingli, Thomas Cranmer, and John Wesley likewise taught perpetual virginity. On the other hand, John Calvin's view was more ambiguous: we cannot know what happened to Mary, Calvin believed, yet the Bible does not contradict the possibility of her lifelong sexual abstinence (www.ccel.org/ccel/calvin/calcom31.toc.html, *Commentary on Matt.* 1:25).

2. She is not, of course, the mother of all three persons of the Trinity. That would be the heresy of goddess worship. But Mary certainly is the physical mother of the second person of the Trinity (God the Son), ever since He came down to us and was born as a real man, Jesus of Nazareth.

Chapter 6: Thomas

1. Earlychristianwritings.com, Patterson and Meyer, *Gospel of Thomas* 37, 98.

2. See the introduction for remarks on the debate about how to define "Christians" in the ancient context.

3. ccel.org/ccel/mcclure, *Pilgrimage of Etheria* 30, 32.

Chapter 7: James

1. Earlychristianwritings.com, Patterson and Meyer, *Gospel of Thomas* 12.

2. Earlychristianwritings.com, R. Cameron, *Secret Book of James.*

3. A bishop's chair in the ancient church was called a *cathedra*, from which we get the word cathedral. The use of a distinct chair for a church's leading pastor must have emerged by the late second century, because around AD 200 Tertullian claimed that an observer could find "the very thrones of the apostles . . . still pre-eminent in their places" (ANF, vol. 3, *Prescription Against Heretics* 36). Soon the practice of seating the bishop on an elevated chair became universal in the churches. Great preachers such as Augustine of Hippo sat with Holy Scripture open in their laps while the congregation stood and listened. Some ancient Jewish synagogues (e.g., at Delos in Greece or Dura Europos in Syria) also featured a prominent chair for the authoritative leader, known as the "seat of Moses." Jesus even used this terminology in Matthew 23:2, though it was probably just a metaphorical description in the first-century context.

Chapter 9: Peter

1. Some early church fathers claimed that Peter was already in Rome at this time. For example, Jerome writes that in the year 42, Peter, "after having been bishop of the church of Antioch and having preached to

the Dispersion . . . pushed on to Rome in the second year of Claudius to overthrow Simon Magus, and held the sacerdotal chair there for twenty-five years" (NPNF2, vol. 3, *Lives of Illustrious Men* 1). Eusebius likewise states that "during the reign of Claudius [AD 41–54], the all-good and gracious Providence, which watches over all things, led Peter, that strongest and greatest of the apostles, and the one who on account of his virtue was the speaker for all the others, to Rome" (NPNF2, vol. 1, *C.H.* 2.14.6). But if this were true, it seems rather strange that Paul's letter to the Romans, written in 57, does not mention Peter in the extensive greetings of chapter 16. We will have to examine all the evidence to determine exactly when—or even if—Peter arrived in Rome. It is also possible that Peter was in and out of Rome at various times, potentially over a twenty-five-year period between the early 40s and the late 60s. As far as his presence in Antioch, we know he was there at least once in the late 40s, though we don't know exactly what he was doing. Yet that hasn't stopped the people of Antakya, Turkey, from venerating a church carved into the side of a mountain as the very spot where St. Peter preached his first sermon in Antioch!

2. The actual arguments are too complex to lay out here, since we want to focus primarily on the postbiblical evidence—the period "after Acts." However, Moody Publishers and other conservative presses have published many books that do an admirable job of describing the authorship debates surrounding the Petrine epistles. I have especially benefited from the work of Karen H. Jobes on 1 Peter (2005) and Gene L. Green on Jude and 2 Peter (2008) in the *Baker Exegetical Commentary on the New Testament*.

3. The scribe for 1 Peter was Silvanus (5:12), but we do not know who functioned in that role for Peter's second epistle. The problem of different Greek styles is not something just noticed by modern commentators. The church father Jerome noted that "the second [epsitle of Peter], on account of its difference from the first in style, is considered by many not to be by him" (NPNF2, vol. 3, *Lives of Illustrious Men* 1).

4. Modern Bible translations often use the expression "dress yourself" to describe what Peter did for himself during his youth, but which others would do for him in his old age. The Greek verb *zonnumi* literally means "to gird or wrap in a band or belt," which probably doesn't imply putting on clothes in this context. It instead refers to being put in bonds or chains, and might even mean being wrapped in flammable clothing to be burned alive (a Roman practice that is attested by several ancient sources). Therefore, it is at least possible that Peter was not only nailed to a wooden cross at his death but set on fire. This would fit with what is recorded about Nero's persecution of the Christians in his circus and gardens.

5. Earlychristianwritings.com/actspeter.html.

6. Tertullian.org/fathers/hegesippus_03_book3.htm, end of section II.

7. Soon after the explanation from "Hegesippus," Jerome advances the same idea (NPNF2, vol. 3, *Lives of Illustrious Men* 1). These works are from two hundred years after the *Acts of Peter*, so they probably represent a later attempt to put a more spiritual spin on the tradition of Peter's inverted crucifixion.

8. Penelope.uchicago.edu/Thayer/E/Roman/Texts/Tacitus/home. html, Annals 15.44.

9. Earlychristianwritings.com/text/ascension.html.

10. A Corinthian ministry is not widely attested for Peter, but a century after his lifetime, the local bishop at Corinth appears to have believed it. This would certainly explain the existence of a faction devoted to Peter in that church (1 Cor. 1:12; 3:22).

11. The complete silence in the book of Acts about Peter's presence in Rome suggests Luke may not have had much information about Peter's work there. This would be more likely if Peter's visits to Rome were intermittent, as opposed to him being a permanent fixture whom all the Roman Christians revered. At the very least, we would surmise that Peter wasn't present in the city during the late 50s when Paul sent his epistle to the Romans with many personal greetings, nor in the very early 60s, when Luke was in Rome along with Paul. Presumably these two missionaries would have interacted with Peter if he had been there, and Luke would have left some record of it. Alternatively, it is possible that the falling-out between Peter and Paul described in Galatians 2:11–14 created such a relational rift between the two men that they agreed to work in separate ministry circles. As we saw in our chapter on James, the records of Jewish-Christianity seem to preserve ancient memories of tensions between the Petrine and Pauline perspectives on salvation. However, the two epistles of Peter reveal that his theology was actually very similar to Paul's; and 2 Peter 3:15 even refers to Paul as "our beloved brother." Luke's silence about Peter's work in Rome therefore suggests Peter wasn't in the capital at the same time as Paul—at least not until after Acts was written in 62.

12. See Matthew 27:57–60 and John 19:38–42 on the careful and respectful burial of Jesus. Further evidence of the early Christians' insistence on obtaining the bodies of their revered dead can be found in the letter that Ignatius of Antioch wrote on his way to martyrdom in Rome, only fifty years after the time of Peter. Ignatius says he hopes the wild beasts in the arena will completely devour him so he won't be a bother to anyone trying to bury him afterward (ANF, vol. 1, *Letter to the Romans* 4; see also *Martyrdom of Polycarp* 17–18). Sometimes the Christians even resorted to nighttime theft or bribery to gain custody of their martyrs' mortal remains (NPNF2, vol. 1, *C.H.* 5.1.61).

13. Caius wrote this statement in response to a man named Proclus, who, in an attempt to bolster the apostolic validity of a certain Asian type of theology, had been celebrating the presence of Philip's tomb in Hierapolis (as mentioned in our previous chapter). Caius then trumps his opponent with the argument that Rome has an ever better set of

apostolic shrines in its vicinity. We can see that in this era, famous graves were an important source of local Christian identity—as well as a cause for rivalry!

14. If you would like to see the tombs of the necropolis and the original site of Peter's monument, the Vatican maintains a very nice website with a multimedia presentation that allows a visitor to take a virtual tour of the sacred place: www.vatican.va/various/basiliche/necropoli/scavi_english.html. (Keep in mind that this burial ground was originally in the open air, though it now lies deep beneath the layers of later ecclesiastical construction.) For those who have the opportunity to visit Rome, special permission to tour the necropolis can be requested by following the directions provided online by the Vatican Excavations Office (Ufficio Scavi).

Chapter 10: Paul

1. For this reconstruction, I am indebted to one of the best researched and most erudite books I have ever encountered on early Christian Rome: Peter Lampe, *From Paul to Valentinus* (Minneapolis: Fortress, 2003).

2. Among the many outlandish complaints made by the first-century satirical writer Juvenal, he bemoans the presence of money-hungry Jews around the Capena Gate through which the Appian Road ran. Though formerly known as a frequent haunt of one of Rome's original kings, the area is now, Juvenal says, overrun with foreign interlopers (*Satire* 3.10–16).

3. Pliny, *Natural History* 19.1.

4. This epistle may not have been written by the actual Clement but by an unknown author writing in his name. Whatever the case, it represents the view of Paul's final end that was current in Rome around the turn of the first century.

5. Earlychristianwritings.com/actspeter.html, M.R. James, *Vercelli Acts 1*.

6. Most liberal scholars do not even think there was a release. Because the Pastoral Epistles are not considered authentic, there is no evidence—at least not prior to Eusebius in the fourth century—for any Pauline ministry after his Roman imprisonment described in Acts 28. According to this hypothesis, Paul was simply executed by the imperial authorities soon after his two-year house arrest in Rome.

7. Earlychristianwritings.com/actspaul.html, M.R. James, *Martyrdom 2*.

8. The charge of opposing Caesar by claiming Jesus as the true King goes back to the very beginning of the Christian faith. John 19:12 says, "Pilate sought to release [Jesus], but the Jews cried out, 'If you release this man, you are not Caesar's friend. Everyone who makes himself a king opposes Caesar.'" Along the same lines, in Acts 17:7 the Jews formed a mob of ruffians who accused the Christians of "acting against the decrees of Caesar, saying that there is another king, Jesus."

9. Gutenberg.org/ebooks/6400, *Lives of the Twelve Caesars*, Nero 16.

10. In 2 Timothy 4:13, Paul requests a cloak and some books and papers that he left in Troas, a city on the Aegean. It is hard to imagine he was referring to items from seven years earlier, the last time he was in Troas. Apparently Paul had returned there more recently. Furthermore, he had visited Miletus (2 Tim. 4:20) and Crete (Titus 1:5), and he spent a winter at the Greek city of Nicopolis (Titus 3:12). These locations all attest to Paul's presence in the Aegean Sea region. By stationing himself in Nicopolis on the western coast of Greece during the winter of 63–64, Paul was in excellent position to reach Italy after the fire broke out the next summer. A short hop across the Ionian Sea would have brought him to the Appian Road leading straight into Rome. The decision to winter at Nicopolis—a city not otherwise attested for Paul's ministry—suggests he may have already had a return trip to Italy in mind.

11. Eusebius is the first historical figure to mention Paul's release and subsequent rearrest. However, he interprets the "first defense" of 2 Timothy 4:16 as a reference to the two-year house arrest in Rome, whereas I follow many modern scholars in seeing it as an initial hearing during Paul's second round of judicial proceedings. Even so, Eusebius provides excellent corroboration of the fact that Paul was released to embark on further ministry before being rearrested and executed. The phrase "it is said" indicates Eusebius was repeating an earlier tradition that he had received.

12. A slightly different hypothesis is advanced by the most comprehensive book in English on Paul's final days—a book with whose conclusions I have often, though not always, found myself in agreement. Harry W. Tajra argues in *The Martyrdom of St. Paul* (Tübingen, Germany: Mohr Siebeck 1994; repr. Eugene, OR: Wipf & Stock, 2010) that Paul returned to Rome just before the Great Fire, where he found himself caught up in the strife that swirled between three groups: the formal Jewish leadership in the city, the Jewish-Christians who had not entirely separated from the synagogues, and the Gentile Christians who admired Paul. At the instigation of the Jewish leaders, Paul was arrested by the imperial authorities and executed on charges of treason. This event propelled Christianity into the consciousness of Nero and his magistrates, at which point the religion's entirely negative reputation prompted the emperor to target the Christians as his scapegoats when the fire broke out in the summer of 64. (See Tajra, 27–32 and 79–84.) By way of assessment, I will say that I do not find this reconstruction entirely improbable, yet I prefer to suggest the fire was the reason for Paul's return to Rome—otherwise, why else did he go back? It is furthermore unnecessary to view the Jewish leadership as the main reason why Paul was rearrested, since the pagan authorities and the populace alike already hated Christianity without any need for prompting by Jewish accusations. Nero's cruelty, paranoia, and egomania provide ample reason for the apprehension and execution of Peter and Paul on charges of treason, as well as for the vicious pogrom against the Christians that ensued after the fire. In the end, though, we cannot know exactly what year Paul returned to Rome, nor the exact circumstances that led to his rearrest by Nero's court officials. Tajra's reconstruction may in fact be correct.

13. Penelope.uchicago.edu/Thayer/E/Roman/Texts/Tacitus/home. html, *Annals* 15.44.

14. Earlychristianwritings.com/actspaul.html, M.R. James, *Martyrdom* 5.

15. The terminology used in the text, "to give the seal in the Lord," is associated in Pauline thought with the gift of the Holy Spirit (2 Cor. 1:22; Eph. 1:13; 4:30), a gift that is provided through baptism (1 Cor. 12:13; see also Acts 2:38). The phrase "seal in Christ" appears earlier in the *Acts of Paul* (chapter 25) as Christian baptism, so it is probably what is meant here when Titus and Luke offer it to the newly converted Roman officials.

16. Though this practice may sound strange to some readers, it was based on biblical precedent: "And God was doing extraordinary miracles by the hands of Paul, so that even handkerchiefs or aprons that had touched his skin were carried away to the sick, and their diseases left them and the evil spirits came out of them" (Acts 19:11–12).

17. The alternate martyrdom location at an estate called Aquae Salvias is mentioned in the sixth-century Greek text called the *Acts of the Holy Apostles Peter and Paul* (newadvent.org/fathers/0815.htm). The head-bouncing story that gave the place its current name of "Three Fountains" (Tre Fontane) comes from a late medieval travel guide called the *Marvels of the City of Rome* (*Mirabiliana* 1.5). These texts are too far removed from the original events to be of much historical value.

ACKNOWLEDGMENTS

I gratefully acknowledge the help of
two scholars far more erudite than I,
Michael Graves and Paul Hartog,
whose insights into the manuscript
were of great help to me,
and whose friendship is
an even greater blessing.

I also acknowledge the
fine editorial work of Pam Pugh,
whose labors helped make this book
worthy to bear the name of the
great institution where I serve.

THE MOODY
BIBLE COMMENTARY

THE

MOODY

BIBLE COMMENTARY

A ONE VOLUME COMMENTARY *on the* WHOLE BIBLE
by the FACULTY *of* MOODY BIBLE INSTITUTE

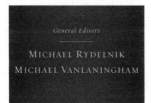

General Editors

MICHAEL RYDELNIK
MICHAEL VANLANINGHAM

978-0-8024-2867-7

MOODY
Publishers™

From the Word *to* Life

www.MoodyPublishers.com

From the Word **to Life**

Moody Radio produces and delivers compelling programs filled with biblical insights and creative expressions of faith that help you take the next step in your relationship with Christ.

You can hear Moody Radio on 36 stations and more than 1,500 radio outlets across the U.S. and Canada. Or listen on your smartphone with the Moody Radio app!

www.moodyradio.org